CliffsNotes™

Hamlet

By Carla Lynn Stockton

IN THIS BOOK

- Discover William Shakespeare and his writing
- Preview an Introduction to the Play
- Explore themes, character development, and recurring images in the Critical Commentaries
- Savor in-depth Character Analyses
- Understand the play better through the Critical Essays
- Reinforce what you learn with the CliffsNotes Review
- Find additional information to further your study in the CliffsNotes Resource Center and online at www.cliffsnotes.com

Wiley Publishing, Inc.

About the Author

Carla Lynn Stockton, B.A., M.A., C.A.S., is a veteran teacher of English and Drama. In 1995, after a month of study through Roehampton University at the Royal Shakespeare Company in Stratford-Upon-Avon, she cofounded and codirected VOICES, a semi-professional theater company dedicated to theater education and education through theater. Today Ms. Stockton is the Education and Development Director for Bagelfish Productions, LLC, in Connecticut.

Publisher's Acknowledgments

Editorial

Project Editor: Kathleen M. Cox
Acquisitions Editor: Greg Tubach
Copy Editor: Corey Dalton
Editorial Assistant: Carol Strickland
Glossary Editors: The editors and staff of Webster's New World Dictionaries

Composition

Indexer: York Production Services, Inc.
Proofreader: York Production Services, Inc.
Wiley Indianapolis Composition Services

CliffsNotes™ ***Hamlet***

Published by:
Wiley Publishing, Inc.
111 River Street
Hoboken, NJ 07030
www.wiley.com

Library of Congress Cataloging-in-Publication Data
Stockton, Carla Lynn, 1947-
CliffsNotes Shakespeare's Hamlet / by Carla Lynn Stockton.
p. cm.
Includes index.
ISBN 0-7645-8603-3 (alk. paper)
1. Shakespeare, William, 1564-1616. Hamlet--Examinations--Study guides. I. Title: Shakespeare's Hamlet. II. Title.

PR2807 .S758 2000
822.3'3--dc21 00-038862
CIP

ISBN: 0-7645-8603-3
Printed in the United States of America
10 9
1O/RV/RQ/QS/IN
Published by Wiley Publishing, Inc., Indianapolis, IN
Published simultaneously in Canada

Table of Contents

How to Use This Book

This CliffsNotes study guide on Shakespeare's *Hamlet* supplements the original literary work, giving you background information about the author, an introduction to the work, a graphical character map, critical commentaries, expanded glossaries, and a comprehensive index, all for you to use as an educational tool that will allow you to better understand *Hamlet*. This study guide was written with the assumption that you have read *Hamlet*. Reading a literary work doesn't mean that you immediately grasp the major themes and devices used by the author; this study guide will help supplement your reading to be sure you get all you can from Shakespeare's *Hamlet*. CliffsNotes Review tests your comprehension of the original text and reinforces learning with questions and answers, practice projects, and more. For further information on William Shakespeare and *Hamlet*, check out the CliffsNotes Resource Center.

CliffsNotes provides the following icons to highlight essential elements of particular interest:

Reveals the underlying themes in the work.

Helps you to more easily relate to or discover the depth of a character.

Uncovers elements such as setting, atmosphere, mystery, passion, violence, irony, symbolism, tragedy, foreshadowing, and satire.

Enables you to appreciate the nuances of words and phrases.

Don't Miss Our Web Site

Discover classic literature as well as modern-day treasures by visiting the CliffsNotes Web site at `www.cliffsnotes.com`. You can obtain a quick download of a CliffsNotes title, purchase a title in print form, browse our catalog, or view online samples.

LIFE AND BACKGROUND OF THE AUTHOR

The following abbreviated biography of William Shakespeare is provided so that you might become more familiar with his life and the historical times that possibly influenced his writing. Read this Life and Background of the Author section and recall it when reading Shakespeare's *Hamlet*, thinking of any thematic relationship between Shakespeare's work and his life.

Personal Background

Scholars know little about Shakespeare the Man, but significant evidence exists to suggest that Shakespeare the Writer/Producer/Actor/Director achieved success as an entrepreneur, and that he possessed an acute sense of what makes good theater and good entertainment. The very prosperous middle class that spawned him allowed William Shakespeare to parlay his sensitive understanding of entertainment into a financial success.

Shakespeare's father, a landowner who raised sheep, was a well-respected guild member in Stratford-Upon-Avon, a major midlands trade center at the heart of England. He attained public office before reaching his twentieth birthday and rose to the position of High Lord Mayor before his son William left for London in 1592. The prestige and respect that the elder Mr. Shakespeare earned in his lifetime afforded him and his descendants a coat of arms in 1596—a veritable promotion from commoner to peer of the realm, gentry status. William Shakespeare was heir to entitlement.

Born in 1564, William was the eldest son of John and Mary Shakespeare. Though no records corroborate, Shakespeare undoubtedly attended Edward VI grammar school, established in 1543 for the sons of the landed gentry of the community. The curriculum would have versed the young Shakespeare in Latin, Greek, Hebrew, French, and some German; he would have read the Classics and been well familiarized with the writings of Aristotle, Plautus, Cicero, and others, and he would have been schooled in Italian poetry and art.

In 1582, William Shakespeare's name appears on a marriage certificate at Trinity Church along with his wife Anne Hathaway, the daughter of a landowner in nearby Shottery. The two became parents to Susanna seven months later. A birth certificate in 1585 naming Shakespeare father to twins Hamnet and Judith provides the last record of the life he led before he left for London to join a theater company. As far as anyone can tell, Shakespeare left for London in 1585 or 1586, and his name disappears from all records for several years.

In 1592, a theater critic contemporary of Shakespeare's wrote a scathing review of a play that lists William Shakespeare as a weak and unpromising player. From then on, however, the existing reviews are increasingly positive and increasingly about Shakespeare's writing rather than his acting. By 1595 Shakespeare had attained enough of a stronghold in the London theater world to become a shareholder in the Lord Chamberlain's Men, a popular London acting company.

In 1596, the same year that his father achieved peerage, Shakespeare's only son Hamnet died. The following year William Shakespeare returned to Stratford and bought the grandest house in town, an elegant estate called New Place. Back in London, Shakespeare participated in the design and construction of the Globe Theater, which opened on Bankside in 1599.

Shakespeare's reputation and success grew each year. After his father died in 1601 and he inherited the house now known as "The (Shakespeare) Birthplace," he bought into the construction of the Blackfriars Theater, one of the first indoor theaters designed and built by contemporary architect and set designer Inigo Jones. James I, King of England, patented The Chamberlain's Men in 1603, and the company renamed itself The King's Men. As such, the players mounted approximately twelve productions a year at court. By 1609, they had moved permanently to the Blackfriars Theater where they performed year-round. In 1610, Shakespeare purchased a large townhouse in London but returned to live permanently in Stratford

After his death in 1616, Shakespeare was buried in Holy Trinity Church, Stratford-upon-Avon. His daughters, Judith Quiney and Susanna Hall, inherited New Place, his birthplace, and all his various London and Stratford properties; Anne Hathaway inherited his "second best bed."

INTRODUCTION TO THE PLAY

The following Introduction section is provided solely as an educational tool and is not meant to replace the experience of your reading the work. Read the Introduction and A Brief Synopsis to enhance your understanding of the work and to prepare yourself for the critical thinking that should take place whenever you read any work of fiction or nonfiction. Keep the List of Characters and Character Map at hand so that as you read the original literary work, if you encounter a character about whom you're uncertain, you can refer to the List of Characters and Character Map to refresh your memory.

Notes on Composition

The first clear reference to what we know as Shakespeare's *Hamlet* appears in the Stationers' Register, 26 July 1602, as a play called *The Revenge of Hamlet Prince [of] Denmark.* In that article, the author says the play was "lately acted by the Lord Chamberlain his servants". In his list of London plays published in 1598, Francis Meres makes no mention of any play called *Hamlet,* but a note in Gabriel Harvey's edition of Speght's *Chaucer* (published in 1598) does mention the play *Hamlet.* Since scholars question the date of the actual writing of that note, most of them agree that Shakespeare published Hamlet after 1601 and before 1603. *The First Folio,* in 1623, categorized Shakespeare's plays as Comedies, Histories, and Tragedies. Shakespeare wrote the great tragedies—excluding *Romeo and Juliet,* which is not, strictly speaking, a true tragedy—between 1601 and 1606, and apparently *Hamlet* was written first. Shakespeare closely followed *Hamlet* with *Othello* (1604), *King Lear* (1605/6), and *Macbeth* (1606), but a number of experts in Bardology (the study of Shakespeare, who is known as The Bard of Avon) believe that *Hamlet* represents the best of Shakespeare's work. It is the perfect play.

The Texts

Scholars base modern editions of *Hamlet* on the three versions of the play published by 1623. Two of the versions appeared while the author was alive; the third surfaced seven years after his death.

The First Quarto (so named because the play was printed on paper that was folded in four parts) is difficult to read. It contains 240 more lines than in the next version (the First Folio), but it has merit because it represents the first publication of the actual stage version of the play.

In some cases, the writing in the First Quarto is so amateurishly unpolished as to make the experts believe that the First Quarto edition is poorly done and fraught with mistakes, designed essentially as an acting script marked over and edited by an actor.

The Second Quarto edition of *Hamlet,* published in 1604, used a more finely tuned edition as its basis. John Heminge and Henry Condell, members of Shakespeare's company, compiled the First Folio by combining the Second Quarto text with updated stage manager's notes. Thus, scholars base modern texts largely—if indirectly—on the text of the Second Quarto.

The Source

Theater has always been a collaborative art. In Shakespeare's time, a repertory company could not expect a playwright to write in a vacuum. The nature of the schedule, in which a new play could be commissioned weekly, required playwrights to collaborate. English playwrights in the late 16th and early 17th centuries freely borrowed material from one another and shared criticisms and edits. *Hamlet,* like the other great works attributed to Shakespeare, definitely presents Shakespeare's work, but also showcases many contributions by actors, managers, prompters, and so forth, who all knew what parts of a play to leave in or take out.

Like the Greeks, Elizabethan and Jacobean audiences attended the theater to watch plays they had seen often or which were based on stories as familiar to them as their own family histories. Accordingly, Shakespeare based his *Hamlet* on a popular Scandivian saga that had existed for at least a hundred years in one form or another, and which actors all over Europe had performed in earlier manifestations as early as the 1550's.

Newington Butts featured the Lord Chamberlain's Men in *Hamlet,* an earlier revenge play, directed by Henslowe, on June 9, 1594. Scholars commonly call this *Hamlet* the *Ur-Hamlet* and believe the author to be Shakespeare's brilliant contemporary Thomas Kyd. Neither a copy of the *Ur-Hamlet* nor concrete evidence that Kyd actually wrote the play exist, but the story of *Hamlet* does bear a strong resemblance to Kyd's masterpiece *The Spanish Tragedy,* which many scholars believe to be a perfected version of the *Ur-Hamlet.*

Both Kyd and Shakespeare would have read Saxo Grammaticus' *Historia Danica,* an anthology of legends and myths from the Norselands, translated and popularized in French by Belleforest in 1570. Thomas Pavier issued an English translation of Belleforest's version of the story of *Hamlet* in 1608 under the title *The Hystorie of Hamblet.*

In Belleforest's retelling of the old story, which takes place in the days before Christianity found its way to either Denmark or England, the public knows of King Hamlet's murder, and the new King claims he killed King Hamlet while acting in defense of the Queen. Hamlet is a youngster who can only pretend to take care of himself. Although he admires truth, he cannot see beyond his vindictive spirit and exhibits exceeding cruelty. In this version, Hamlet goes to Britain where he marries and stays with his wife, the daughter of the English king, for a full year. News of Hamlet's death reaches the King of Denmark, and he throws a party to celebrate, but Hamlet appears as the party gets under way. This early Hamlet takes immediate action: he gets the court drunk and sets fire to the palace, immediately killing the King.

The play on which Shakespeare based *Hamlet* was a bloody tale full of sound and fury with crude and savage overtones. Though the bloodshed remains in Shakespeare's version, he refined the play, making it poetic and full of thought-provoking ruminations on the meaning of life, death, eternity, relationships, hypocrisy, truth, the existence of God and almost anything else that concerns mankind. However, the fact that the Shakespearean character of Hamlet is more refined creates a problem for those who would interpret the play.

Shakespeare wrote the standard revenge play, but in an entirely new form. Revenge tragedy was hugely popular in Shakespeare's day. The revenge play revolved around a hero who was bound to avenge a wrong. Like their models in the Roman tragedy of Seneca, the heroes and villains were dramatically mad, melancholy, violent. The plays were graphic, bloody. Shakespeare, being an original thinker, placed refinements in his work, creating new tensions and increasing some of the old questions.

Were the play a true revenge play, Hamlet would act sooner. He would dispatch the King at the start, with the rest of the play elaborating upon what transpires after Claudius' death. By not acting more promptly, Hamlet leaves us pondering his true motivation. Hamlet has every opportunity to kill the unguarded King, yet Claudius lives. Shakespeare's Hamlet's obstacles are not physical, and within this fact lies the first rub for critics and interpreters. Hamlet's actual obstacles depend largely on the culture from which the interpreter comes; obstacles that seem obvious to modern readers/audiences never occurred to readers/audiences of the 16th century.

The fact that people need CliffsNotes to understand Shakespeare's work would undoubtedly appall him. Shakespeare wrote for a popular, vibrant theater that attracted people because of its energy and its raw entertainment value. The same audience who attended bearbaiting or public executions went to see Shakespeare's plays. They were not a highbrow crowd; they just wanted to hear a protagonist agonize with pretty words and sexual innuendo over the human dilemma, and they went to see blood and destruction manifest on stage.

The English crowd loved gore. Though they seem to have enjoyed the sight of dogs mauling bears to death and executioners drawing and quartering traitors, they especially enjoyed staged mayhem. They loved the techniques Shakespeare's technical experts used to simulate blood gushing from stabbed characters; they loved the way a good showman could make battles or love scenes or illnesses seem absolutely real even though the audience could leave assured that what they had just seen was fiction. Shakespeare's theatrical offerings were as popular in his day as television is today; Shakespeare's theater was the television of its day. If Shakespeare were alive today, he would probably be writing for *Dawson's Creek* or *Melrose Place.*

Significance

Scholars universally recognize Hamlet as the one character in the Shakespeare canon that best exemplifies Shakespeare's ability to express the universal awareness of human existence. He personifies Shakespeare's genius and, by the very nature of his enigmatic presence, captures the human imagination better than any other literary character before or since.

Hamlet's dual nature, so recognizable to anyone who has ever been a teenager, ignites immediate empathy. Hamlet is sensitive, poetic, artistic, and loving; he is also a criminal who stabs his friends in the back, treats his young girlfriend callously, and shows no remorse for deliberately murdering an "unseen good old man." Other artists— from intellectual writers to pop culture songsters—allude to no other play more often. They also quote, mimic, and emulate no character more than Hamlet.

The most enduring thing about *Hamlet,* which keeps the play vibrant for every age, is that no key to understanding the play exists. Viewers can validate all interpretations, justify every answer, and substantiate all possibilities. Fierce debate over *Hamlet's* meaning, the title character's mystery, his mystique, how his life relates to modern man, what his relationships can teach us about human interaction, and more, will forever attend any examination of the play. So long as unanswerable questions persist, the play will captivate us. However, some points of reference to which most critics, actors, directors, and academic interpreters agree do exist.

One given is that, from the start, Hamlet has a clear imperative to act on his medieval blood feud: to avenge his father's death by killing King Claudius. His emotions tear him in two. On the one hand, he possesses the basic male need to assert his manhood and to right grave wrongs. On the other, his Christian, moral knowledge tells him that murder constitutes a sin no matter what the cause.

Hamlet represents the polar opposite of his uncle/father King Claudius. Claudius personifies the Machiavellian villain: he justifies his wrongdoing by aggrandizing the ends his evil produces. He recognizes his own evil and acknowledges his doomed status. Knowing that he will assuredly descend into hell makes Claudius no less eager to commit crime after crime in order to keep his ill-won spoils. The desire to resist hating him moves the audience, and the fact that he is so conversant with his inability to seek absolution keeps him from being one-dimensional. Rather than hate him, we root for his conversion, hoping that he will confess and show contrition. He does not, and we become less and less forgiving. Hamlet is Claudius' antithesis. The Prince knows he owes a debt to his father's commands and to the old order which dictates that he must commit a sinful act. But his fear that the action is wrong paralyzes him. Though the end would justify Hamlet's very existence, it would not justify his defiance of the commandment against murder.

Critics argue that Hamlet's inability to make up his mind makes him a tragic figure. Truthfully, however, Hamlet's "wild and whirling words" are the culprits that imprison him. Like other great Shakespearean tragic heroes, Hamlet must find a way to turn his ideas—the persevering words that never allow him silence—to into action. In *Macbeth,* the hero reverses roles with his wife; she, quick to act, becomes the talker, the thinker, while he becomes the rash one, the man of action. In *King Lear,* madness robs Lear of his words, forcing him to listen, to recognize reality in order to experience his recognition and reversal. But in *Hamlet,* the words control the hero to the end —until he knows that he is dead and can end the discussion and finally act. Like a composer who hears music playing incessantly in his head, Hamlet struggles to swim through a constant stream of words to his death, where he sighs that "The rest is silence."

One difficulty in interpreting *Hamlet* arises out the intimate nature of the obstacles that confront the hero. Most of the conflict Hamlet must overcome results from his internal struggle, not from external obstacles. In addition to all the difficulties that hinder Hamlet from within, however, a fair share of outside impediments also stand in the way of his taking decisive action.

The fact that Claudius holds all the cards and exposes Hamlet "naked" to all Denmark presents an entirely external conflict. The Ghost orders Hamlet to avenge the old king's death, yet no witnesses attest to the fact that King Hamlet did not die of natural causes. King Claudius is the Divine Right monarch and, by killing him, Hamlet will commit high treason and dispatch an emissary from God at the same time. To the world around him, Hamlet seems to be playing out of tune. He is popular and admired by Claudius' Danish subjects, but they have no reason to believe that Claudius is anything but what he says he is, a noble king. If Hamlet knows that his world is "out of joint," that things are not what they appear to be, that "there is something rotten in the State of Denmark," he has no proof and no allies. The King even manipulates Hamlet's own mother and Hamlet's courtship of the fair Ophelia. Except for Horatio, Hamlet is alone.

This CliffsNote is a companion to the play. It cannot serve as a substitute for reading the entire play, watching a live theatrical performance, or viewing the many film versions in theatrical release and on video. Additionally, plays like *Rosencrantz and Guildenstern are Dead; I Hate Hamlet; Words, Words; The Hamlet Machine; Ten Minute Hamlet;* and others offer new insights into *Hamlet* as they present completely new situations using the familiar plot and characters. Even Walt Disney's *The Lion King* takes its basis from *Hamlet* and illuminates Shakespeare's work even as the original illuminates it in return.

(All references to the text are taken from the Cambridge School edition of *Hamlet,* published by Cambridge University Press, 1994.)

A Brief Synopsis

Prince Hamlet is depressed. Having been summoned home to Denmark from school in Germany to attend his father's funeral, he is shocked to find his mother Gertrude already remarried. The Queen has wed Hamlet's Uncle Claudius, the dead king's brother. To Hamlet, the marriage is "foul incest." Worse still, Claudius has had himself crowned King despite the fact that Hamlet was his father's heir to the throne. Hamlet suspects foul play.

When his father's ghost visits the castle, Hamlet's suspicions are confirmed. The Ghost complains that he is unable to rest in peace because he was murdered. Claudius, says the Ghost, poured poison in King Hamlet's ear while the old king napped. Unable to confess and find salvation, King Hamlet is now consigned, for a time, to spend his days in Purgatory and walk the earth by night. He entreats Hamlet to avenge his death, but to spare Gertrude, to let Heaven decide her fate.

Hamlet vows to affect madness—puts "an antic disposition on"—to wear a mask that will enable him to observe the interactions in the castle, but finds himself more confused than ever. In his persistent confusion, he questions the Ghost's trustworthiness. What if the Ghost is not a true spirit, but rather an agent of the devil sent to tempt him? What if killing Claudius results in Hamlet's having to relive his memories for all eternity? Hamlet agonizes over what he perceives as his cowardice because he cannot stop himself from thinking. Words immobilize Hamlet, but the world he lives in prizes action.

In order to test the Ghost's sincerity, Hamlet enlists the help of a troupe of players who perform a play called *The Murder of Gonzago* to which Hamlet has added scenes that recreate the murder the Ghost described. Hamlet calls the revised play *The Mousetrap,* and the ploy proves a success. As Hamlet had hoped, Claudius' reaction to the staged murder reveals the King to be conscience-stricken. Claudius leaves the room because he cannot breathe, and his vision is dimmed for want of light. Convinced now that Claudius is a villain, Hamlet resolves to kill him. But, as Hamlet observes, "conscience doth make cowards of us all."

In his continued reluctance to dispatch Claudius, Hamlet actually causes six ancillary deaths. The first death belongs to Polonius, whom Hamlet stabs through a wallhanging as the old man spies on Hamlet and Gertrude in the Queen's private chamber. Claudius punishes Hamlet for Polonius' death by exiling him to England. He has brought Hamlet's school chums Rosencrantz and Guildenstern to Denmark from Germany to spy on his nephew, and now he instructs them to deliver Hamlet into the English king's hands for execution. Hamlet discovers the plot and arranges for the hanging of Rosencrantz and Guildenstern instead. Ophelia, distraught over her father's death and Hamlet's behavior, drowns while singing sad love songs bemoaning the fate of a spurned lover. Her brother, Laertes, falls next.

Laertes, returned to Denmark from France to avenge his father's death, witnesses Ophelia's descent into madness. After her funeral, where he and Hamlet come to blows over which of them loved Ophelia best, Laertes vows to punish Hamlet for her death as well.

Unencumbered by words, Laertes plots with Claudius to kill Hamlet. In the midst of the sword fight, however, Laertes drops his poisoned sword. Hamlet retrieves the sword and cuts Laertes. The lethal poison kills Laertes. Before he dies, Laertes tells Hamlet that because Hamlet has already been cut with the same sword, he too will shortly die. Horatio diverts Hamlet's attention from Laertes for a moment by pointing out that "The Queen falls."

Gertrude, believing that Hamlet's hitting Laertes means her son is winning the fencing match, has drunk a toast to her son from the poisoned cup Claudius had intended for Hamlet. The Queen dies.

As Laertes lies dying, he confesses to Hamlet his part in the plot and explains that Gertrude's death lies on Claudius' head. Finally enraged, Hamlet stabs Claudius with the poisoned sword and then pours the last of the poisoned wine down the King's throat. Before he dies, Hamlet declares that the throne should now pass to Prince Fortinbras of Norway, and he implores his true friend Horatio to accurately explain the events that have led to the bloodbath at Elsinore. With his last breath, he releases himself from the prison of his words: "The rest is silence."

The play ends as Prince Fortinbras, in his first act as King of Denmark, orders a funeral with full military honors for slain Prince Hamlet.

List of Characters

Hamlet, Prince of Denmark The crown prince of Denmark who returns from the university in Wittenberg, Germany, to find his father dead, his mother married to the king's brother Claudius, and Claudius newly self-crowned King.

Claudius, King of Denmark Dead King Hamlet's brother who has usurped the throne and married his sister-in-law.

Gertrude, Queen of Denmark Prince Hamlet's mother, King Hamlet's widow, King Claudius' wife.

The Ghost Spirit of the late King Hamlet, condemned to walk the earth until his soul is cleansed of its sins.

Polonius The elderly Lord Chamberlain, chief counselor to Claudius.

Horatio A commoner, Horatio went to school with Hamlet and remains his loyal best friend.

Laertes A student in Paris, Laertes is Polonius' son and Ophelia's brother; he returns from school because of King Hamlet's death, leaves to go back to Paris, and then returns again after his own father's murder.

Ophelia Daughter of Polonius, sister of Laertes, Ophelia is beloved of Hamlet.

Rosencrantz and Guildenstern Classmates of Hamlet's in Wittenberg. Claudius summons them to Elsinore to spy on Prince Hamlet.

Fortinbras King of Norway, bound to avenge his father's death by the Danes' hands.

Osric Affected courtier who plays a minor role as the King's messenger and as umpire of the fencing match between Hamlet and Laertes.

Voltimand and Cornelius Danish courtiers who are sent as ambassadors to the Court of Norway.

Marcellus and Barnardo Danish officers on guard at the castle of Elsinore.

Francisco Danish soldier on guard at the castle of Elsinore.

Reynaldo Young man whom Polonius instructs and sends to Paris to observe and report on Laertes' conduct.

Two Clowns (the Gravediggers) Two rustics (identified as clowns) who dig Ophelia's grave.

Character Map

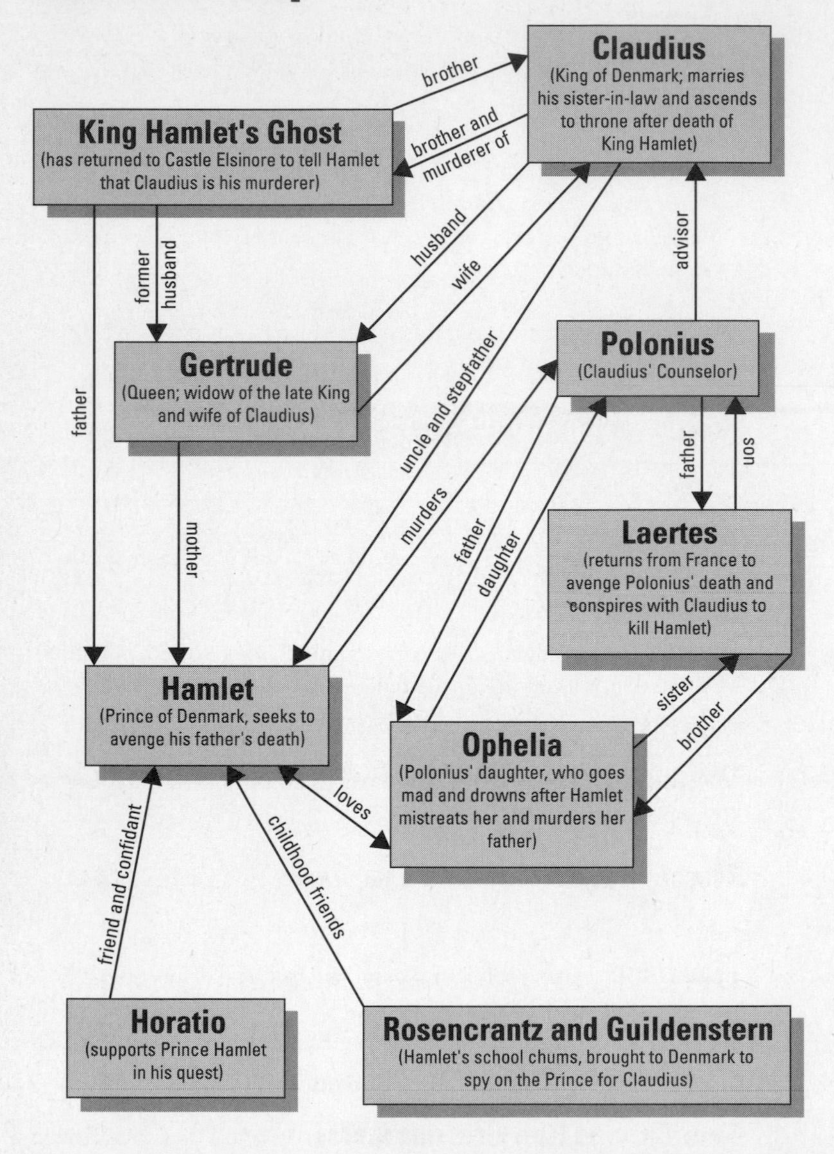

CRITICAL COMMENTARIES

The sections that follow provide great tools for supplementing your reading of *Hamlet*. First, in order to enhance your understanding of and enjoyment from reading, we provide quick summaries in case you have difficulty when you read the original literary work. Each summary is followed by commentary: literary devices, character analyses, themes, and so on. Keep in mind that the interpretations here are solely those of the author of this study guide and are used to jumpstart your thinking about the work. No single interpretation of a complex work like *Hamlet* is infallible or exhaustive, and you'll likely find that you interpret portions of the work differently from the author of this study guide. Read the original work and determine your own interpretations, referring to these Notes for supplemental meanings only.

Act I
Scene 1

Summary

On a gun platform atop the battlements of Castle Elsinore, Officer Barnardo arrives to relieve sentinel Francisco of his watch. Barnardo challenges Francisco to identify himself first, and the two exchange small talk about the weather. Francisco complains, "For this relief much thanks, 'tis bitter cold. / And I am sick at heart."

Horatio and Marcellus enter and greet Francisco, identifying themselves as loyal Danish subjects, and Francisco exits. Marcellus asks Barnardo if he has seen "this thing," "this apparition" tonight, and Barnardo assures him that he has seen nothing. Marcellus tells Barnardo that he has invited Horatio to see the Ghost himself, as he trusts Horatio to "approve our eyes and speak to it." Horatio doubts the Ghost will appear, but listens intently as Barnardo prepares to retell the tale of the Ghost's previous visitation.

Before Barnardo can say much, however, the Ghost appears, and Marcellus encourages Horatio to address the spirit. Horatio cannot deny that he, too, sees the Ghost. All three men agree that the Ghost is real; in fact, they recognize it as the "majesty of buried Denmark"—the recently dead King Hamlet. They entreat the Ghost to stay and talk, but it dissolves into the night.

Saying he would not believe had he not seen for himself, Horatio is astounded to have seen the Ghost of King Hamlet dressed in the armor he wore when he conquered old King Fortinbras and defeated the Poles. He finds the king's dress ironic because, at that moment, young Fortinbras—the dead Norwegian king's son and namesake—has just declared war on the Danes, seeking to avenge his father's death and take back the land King Hamlet took from old Fortinbras. Because the Danes are preparing for war against the Norwegians, Barnardo wonders if the Ghost portends doom for the Danes. Horatio shudders, recalling the omens that warned Julius Caesar of his imminent demise.

The Ghost reappears, and Horatio entreats it to stay. The crowing cock trumpets the arrival of morning, however, and Horatio realizes that no erring spirit can stay out in the daylight; they watch the Ghost disappear into the dissolving darkness. Certain that they have seen the Ghost of King Hamlet, they decide to inform Prince Hamlet.

Commentary

The spooky cold that Francisco describes as he and Barnardo exchange posts thoroughly sets the mood of the play, which Yale Professor Maynard Mack describes as "mysterious and equivocal, a mixture of bright surfaces and dark forces where what seems both is and is not."

This scene shows very clearly the problem of discerning between appearance and reality. The Ghost appears, but is it really there? If it is there, is it really a devil assuming the king's regal shape and garments? Distinguishing between truth and illusion is the focal dilemma of Act I and will challenge Hamlet right up to the play's turning point in Scene 4 of Act IV. Barnardo's questioning of Francisco introduces the idea that Hamlet's world is upside-down. Protocol dictates that Francisco should question the newcomer, but here the interloper questions the guard. Francisco's response reinforces the sense of malaise. His "sickness at heart" prefigures the tension of the ensuing tragedy, while the changing of the guard mirrors the tenuousness of the political climate of Denmark—the transition from one king to another and the arrival of the Prince whose rightful place on the throne has been usurped.

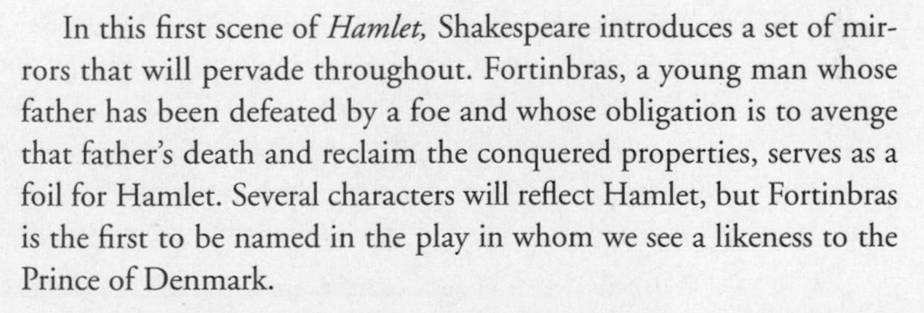

In this first scene of *Hamlet,* Shakespeare introduces a set of mirrors that will pervade throughout. Fortinbras, a young man whose father has been defeated by a foe and whose obligation is to avenge that father's death and reclaim the conquered properties, serves as a foil for Hamlet. Several characters will reflect Hamlet, but Fortinbras is the first to be named in the play in whom we see a likeness to the Prince of Denmark.

Fortinbras has another significance to the play. The first scene presages an important thematic thread in Hamlet, that the passing of the torch from old to young inevitably carries the duty of the young to live up to their elders' expectations. A son must obey a father's instruction, no matter how unreasonable the directive might seem—even if the directive necessitates murder, war, or mayhem. In Scene 1, Horatio explains that, because Young Fortinbras is bent on avenging his father's defeat at Old King Hamlet's hand, all of Denmark prepares for war. A single covenant inexorably propels the events of the play and is the medieval truth that rules Hamlet's life.

Horatio's fear of the Ghost mirrors the prevailing attitude toward witches and ghosts among Elizabethans and Jacobeans. Shakespeare's contemporaries believed in ghosts and closely linked apparitions with their religious fears of the devil's power and hell's dominion on earth. Like witches, ghosts were believed to be agents of an afterlife; unlike witches, however, they were not universally dreaded. While witches always represent the devil, ghosts might actually represent the spirit of God. A ghost could represent angel or devil to the Shakespearean sensibility.

According to the religious precepts of the time, anyone seeing a ghost must identify the ghost's purpose and form. A ghost could be: (1) a hallucination, which was dangerously apt to be engendered by the devil, (2) a restless spirit returned to perform a deed left undone in life, (3) a specter seen as a prediction or warning sent as a gift from God, (4) a spirit returned from beyond the grave by divine permission, or (5) a devil disguised as a dead person. Characters in *Hamlet* test each of these possibilities within the course of the play.

The dead king's armor suggests that the Ghost could be a soldier returned to finish a job left undone, an omen for the troubled country he once ruled and a spirit roaming with divine permission. Horatio dwells on the idea of portents, thus shedding another light on the play to illuminate several other motifs.

Horatio's worrying about the impending attack on Denmark by Fortinbras and his Norwegians reveals another of the many mirrors that layer the play. Fortinbras' honor compels him to attack the established Danes in order to avenge his father, despite the fact that he lacks the funds to pay his warriors. Old Fortinbras and Young Fortinbras, Old Hamlet and Young Hamlet, and Old Polonius and Young Laertes continually exemplify Shakespeare's preoccupation with filial duty and devotion.

Marcellus' reference to Christianity establishes the very Christian context of Hamlet. Marcellus notes that the Ghost stalks away when Heaven is invoked, and also mentions Christmas and "our savior's birth." These comments clearly define the religious perspective of the characters in the play, which reflect Shakespeare's own reputedly Catholic point of view.

Act I, Scene 1, introduces imagery suggesting that Elsinore is itself a prison where impending war and disaster are inevitable, that forces beyond human control threaten all hope of happiness or well-being.

Glossary

unfold yourself to make known or lay open to view, especially in stages or little by little.

most carefully upon your hour exactly when you were expected.

rivals associates or companions in some duty.

liegemen loyal subjects.

pole Polaris, the North Star, long used by navigators as a reliable point of reference.

scholar a person with the necessary knowledge of Latin to exorcise a spirit. This was a common Elizabethan belief.

mark take notice of; heed.

Norway king of Norway.

sledded Polacks the Polish army traveling on sleighs or sleds.

jump precisely.

gross and scope general meaning.

divide distinguish.

prick'd spurred or urged on

seized of put in legal possession of a feudal holding; assigned ownership.

moiety competent sufficient portion.

gaged pledged.

unimproved mettle untested strength, courage, or character

skirts the outer or bordering parts; outskirts, as of a city.

Shark'd gathered indiscriminately; got by fraud or strategems.

lawless resolutes desperadoes.

question subject.

mote speck of dust.

palmy flourishing.

sheeted shrouded.

moist star moon.

precurse sign, indication.

harbingers persons or things that come before to announce or give an indication of what follows; heralds

partisan a broad-bladed weapon with a long shaft carried by foot soldiers, used especially in the 16th century.

extravagant and erring vagrant and wandering (both used in their original Latin sense—a common device used by Shakespeare).

confine prison.

probation proof.

no fairy takes Medieval Europeans believed that fairies stole children.

russet Now, usually a reddish-brown color, but here the warm gray tone of homespun cloth.

Act I
Scene 2

Summary

In a trumpet flourish, Claudius, the new King of Denmark, and his wife Gertrude enter their stateroom in the company of various courtiers, including Prince Hamlet, Claudius' aide Polonius, Polonius' son Laertes, and the ambasadors to Norway Voltemand and Cornelius. Claudius explains that he and Gertrude have chosen to marry immediately after his brother's death because, in light of the encroaching Danish army, the court could not afford excessive grief lest young Fortinbras mistake their mourning for weakness. He dispatches Voltemand and Cornelius to inform young Fortinbras' uncle of the young man's campaign against the Danes. As Claudius is himself, Fortinbras' uncle is brother to the recently dead king and currently controls the throne. Claudius hopes that the old man has the power to stop Fortinbras from carrying out his mission.

Claudius then turns his attention to Laertes, who petitions the King for permission to return to school in France. Claudius confers with Polonius who answers verbosely that he consents to Laertes' wish.

Having dismissed Laertes, the King and Queen both notice Hamlet's dark demeanor, and Hamlet sneers at the King's loving posture. Gertrude and Claudius encourage him to cease grieving and to get on with life. Gertrude asks Hamlet why he seems so particularly affected by his father's death, and Hamlet snaps at her that, unlike his mother and her husband, he has no pretenses. "Seems, Madam? Nay, it is." Hamlet accuses Gertrude of pretending grief and rejoicing in the old king's death. Claudius reminds Hamlet that he is next in line to the throne, and asks him not to return to school in Wittenberg, a request that Gertrude reiterates. Hamlet acquiesces without enthusiasm. Satisfied that they have had their way, Claudius and Gertrude leave Hamlet to his own thoughts.

In his first soliloquy, Hamlet bemoans the fact that he cannot commit suicide. He wishes that his physical self might just cease to exist, "melt, / Thaw, and resolve itself into a dew." He complains that his religion prohibits suicide and claims that he would sooner die than continue watching his mother engage in her vile incest. These thoughts torment him, but he knows that he can't speak them aloud to anyone.

Horatio, Marcellus, and Barnardo enter, and Hamlet, unguarded with Horatio as with no one else, snidely jokes that King Claudius has sought to save money by using the funeral refreshments to feed his wedding guests. He tells Horatio that his father's memory haunts him. Horatio seizes the opportunity to tell Hamlet about his encounter with the Ghost of the old king. Hamlet agrees to watch that night in case the Ghost walks again.

Commentary

It is significant that Claudius admonishes Hamlet as he addresses him for the first time in the play. Claudius is clearly the antagonist, and he begins his hour upon the stage in a blatantly adversarial role. Were Claudius' demeanor not enough to tell the audience that the two are rivals, Hamlet underscores the discomfort of their relationship by asserting his disgust for the man with his own opening statement.

The key words that exemplify the critical purpose of this scene include "show," "seem," and "play." Cornelius and Voltemand say they will "show our duty." Laertes "came to Denmark to show" his allegiance to King Claudius. Gertrude asks Hamlet, in reference to his "nighted color," "Why seems it so particular with thee?" Hamlet responds to her question by using the word "seems" twice in a single sentence, and he says he cannot pretend, but rather, must be what he is. He then goes on to say that the moods and shapes of grief are true for him. Though his emotions may seem to be those of an actor, he is not acting. Everything in this scene points to the challenge of discerning appearance from reality, a challenge that becomes more pronounced when Horatio tells Hamlet about the appearance of the Ghost.

Claudius' calculating nature becomes immediately apparent. Always conscious of appearances—of what seems to be—he speaks of Gertrude as "our sometime sister, now our queen, / Th'imperial jointress to this warlike state," and then addresses Hamlet as his "cousin Hamlet and my son." He has considered his relationships to the state, to Gertrude, and to Hamlet in all the ways people might perceive them, and man-

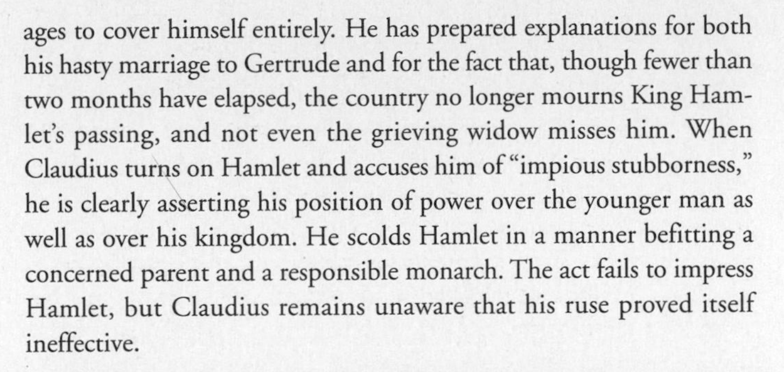
ages to cover himself entirely. He has prepared explanations for both his hasty marriage to Gertrude and for the fact that, though fewer than two months have elapsed, the country no longer mourns King Hamlet's passing, and not even the grieving widow misses him. When Claudius turns on Hamlet and accuses him of "impious stubborness," he is clearly asserting his position of power over the younger man as well as over his kingdom. He scolds Hamlet in a manner befitting a concerned parent and a responsible monarch. The act fails to impress Hamlet, but Claudius remains unaware that his ruse proved itself ineffective.

Claudius further invalidates Hamlet by demeaning the young man's self-image. Accusing Hamlet of possessing "a heart unfortified," "a mind impatient," and an "understanding simple and unschool'd," Claudius defines Hamlet as inadequate to the task of being king. This accusation justifies his own ascension to his brother's throne, despite the fact that the kingship rightfully belongs to the old king's true heir, Hamlet. Every word Claudius chooses, including the condescension implied in his calling Hamlet "my cousin, and my son," reiterates his superiority and complete control.

The incest between Claudius and Gertrude remains at the forefront of Hamlet's mind in this scene. He is most aware of this incest horror, although he suspects other crimes as well. By the end of the play, Hamlet will call Claudius a "murd'rous, damned Dane," and the King will have multiple crimes to answer for. At this moment, however, the medieval English prohibition on sexual intimacy between a brother—albeit a brother-in-law—and sister serves as the primary focus for Hamlet's rage. Though Gertrude's guilt equals Claudius' in this case, Hamlet directs his fury at Claudius and merely mistrusts his mother.

This scene illustrates the actor's challenge in interpreting Gertrude's character. Gertrude's demeanor in this scene is innocent. She genuinely appears to desire happiness for Hamlet, to desire him to stay and be her dutiful son. Seemingly naive and ingenuous, she contrasts starkly with Claudius, who calculates his every word and move to have an effect on his assemblage. If she is less forthright and honest than she appears here, Shakespeare gives no hint. However, as the play unfolds, we increasingly question Gertrude's innocence. In order to make the portrayal believable, the actress must commit to whether Gertrude is playing a role or whether she is genuine.

The disparity between appearance and reality becomes a pervasive thematic motif in *Hamlet.* The Ghost in Scene 1 established the lack of clear lines between the real and the perceived, but the web of deceit and bewilderment in this scene casts a shadow that will hover over the breadth of the play. In his response to Gertrude's supplication that he abandon his grief, Hamlet assures her that he is not one to make "shows of grief . . . that a man might play." Hamlet asserts that he is not merely costumed in his black attire, nor is he prone to dramatic sighs or profuse weeping. He is genuinely grieved and honestly critical of Gertrude's and Claudius' callousness toward the loss of their husband and brother. To Hamlet, all others are making show.

Hamlet's preoccupation with hypocrisy surfaces more profoundly in his first soliloquy. The fact that his mother has joined in an incestuous union with her husband's brother less than a month after his father's death overwhelms Hamlet. A simple beast without the reasoning skills of a human being would have shown more respect for a dead mate, moans Hamlet. Worse yet, Hamlet must question her judgment. Hamlet sees Claudius as a satyr—a beast-man driven by his appetites—whereas Old Hamlet was Hyperion, the sun god himself. How can he trust a woman who would trade a god for a goat? In addition to his cynicism toward women, Hamlet's self-portrait begins to emerge in this soliloquy. When he says that his Uncle Claudius corresponds to his father, King Hamlet, no more "Than I to Hercules," Hamlet discloses his pacifistic demeanor. Hercules was a warrior who acted on impulse and charged enthusiastically into battles without questioning the ideology of the fight. Unlike Hercules, Hamlet drowns in words and perpetually struggles toward understanding.

Knowing his weakness, Hamlet decries his inability to commit suicide, revealing his devotion to the laws of Shakespeare's religion. Hamlet refers to Gertrude's marriage to Claudius as incestuous, though history and cultural practices often encourage marriage between a widow and her brother-in-law. Elizabethan laws had only recently been changed to ban such unions. Hamlet's pain and embarrassment over his mother's incest—a marriage that besmirches her entire culture—is great enough to make him long for the comfort of death but not great enough to allow him to reject "His canon 'gainst self slaughter."

When Barnardo, Marcellus, and Horatio tantalize Hamlet with news of the Ghost, Hamlet excitedly questions them as to the details of the

sighting and asserts his absolute surety that the Ghost is "honest" rather than a "goblin dam'd." Horatio contradicts his own earlier observation that the old king was angry by telling Hamlet that the Ghost seemed clothed "More / In sorrow." The Ghost's misery reinforces Hamlet's belief that the Ghost is in earnest. As his interchange with Horatio illustrates, Hamlet's sardonic sense of humor disguises his own aching melancholy and nagging suspicion that some "foul play" is afoot.

Glossary

in one brow of woe Everyone in the kingdom ought to mourn.

jointress a woman who has been given an interest for life in her deceased husband's estate; here, a partner.

weak supposal poor opinion.

importing concerning.

ourself royal plural, used throughout the King's speeches.

gait progress.

delated articles detailed provisions set forth in their instructions.

pardon permission.

cousin kinsman. This word was used for any near relation; here it would refer to nephew.

sun a pun on son, again indicating Hamlet's dislike of the new relationship between himself and his uncle.

nighted black, signifying deep mourning.

obstinate condolement grief that is contrary to the will of heaven.

corse corpse, dead body.

impart behave.

bend you incline yourself.

Be as ourself in Denmark Claudius is extending to Hamlet all the special privileges and prerogatives belonging to a crowned prince.

rouse draught of liquor, toast.

bruit proclaim.

Fie for shame! an interjection expressing a sense of outraged propriety.

merely entirely, absolutely, altogether.

Hyperion a Titan often identified with the sun god.

satyr in Greek mythology, a woodland diety usually represented as having pointed ears, short horns, the head and body of a man, and the legs of a goat, and as being fond of riotous merriment and lechery.

beteem permit.

Niobe in Greek mythology, a queen of Thebes who, weeping for her slain children, is turned into a stone from which tears continue to flow; hence, an inconsolable woman.

Hercules in Greek and Roman mythology, the son of Zeus, renowned for his strength and courage, especially as shown in his performance of twelve labors imposed on him.

I'll change that name with you I am your servant.

make you from what is the news from?

Season your admiration Moderate your wonder. Shakespeare frequently uses admiration in its original (Latin) sense of wonder.

cap – a – pe fully armed from head to foot.

truncheon a general's baton.

beaver the visor of the helmet, which could be lowered in battle.

sable silver'd black streaked with white.

Act I
Scene 3

Summary

In Polonius' chambers, Laertes prepares to return to school in Paris. He counsels his sister Ophelia to spurn the advances of her suitor, Prince Hamlet. He explains that, to Hamlet, she can never be anything more than a plaything. Hamlet, Laertes tells Ophelia, is of a higher rank than she and cannot choose with whom he will spend his life. To protect her heart and to safeguard her honor, Laertes asserts that Ophelia should reject Prince Hamlet before he deflowers her. Ophelia jokingly chides her brother to be careful lest he be one of those "libertines" who "recks not his own rede" (does not take his own advice).

Polonius enters, and offers Laertes lengthy advice on how to live in Paris; he spouts a string of aphoristic clichés enumerating the shoulds and shouldn'ts of a young man's life. Laertes agrees, telling Polonius that he really must be going, and reminding Ophelia of his directive to her. She promises to take his advice and to lock it safely in her heart. Polonius asks Ophelia what she and Laertes were discussing, and she tells him that Laertes advised her about Prince Hamlet. Polonius launches into his own diatribe on the subject, saying that Hamlet is a red-blooded male who wants her for only one purpose and that she must spurn his advances. Ophelia promises to obey her father and break off her relationship with the Prince.

Commentary

Laertes offers his overprotective advice genuinely, but his tone is that of a prepared speech, and he shows neither real awareness of, nor consideration for, Ophelia's feelings. In fact, he never consults her but rather speaks at her in metaphorical posturing that underscores her feminine inferiority. Shakespeare's choice of blank verse over iambic pentameter for Laertes' speech serves as a stage direction for the actor playing the role. This character is not a man of deep thought or fancy language but rather a pragmatist—a careful courtier more concerned with being correct than with emotional depth. Shakespeare aptly underscores the fact that Laertes is the perfect foil for Hamlet. His rehearsed, political-sounding speech patterns oppose Hamlet's emotional, flowery, and heart-heavy ruminations. He has memorized his speech as if it were taken from his schoolboy copybook, and he shows that he is vain and ordinary with limited intellectual capabilities. This scene begins to reveal how Laertes might be similar to Hamlet—and decidedly different.

Polonius lives in a world of show. His instructions in social etiquette may have ethical substance but lack practical soundness for Laertes. When he speaks to Ophelia, he treats her the way one would expect a man of his time and stature to treat a daughter, as property. A woman should bring honor and fortune to her family, and the image Ophelia projects for him very much concerns Polonius. He is sure that Hamlet would never choose Ophelia to wife. Hence, he amuses himself with off-color allusions to Hamlet's intentions and dashes any hopes she might have that her father would help her make a match. Through Polonius and Laertes, Shakespeare introduces another motif of the play: that self-indulgence and vanity often obscure familial devotion.

Ophelia's dilemma is salient in this scene. Both Laertes and Polonius tell her that the man that she loves is using her, that he will discard her, and that she should not trust her own heart. She is a dutiful daughter. Because her father has taught her to be seen and not heard, she listens and promises to honor the men's wishes. No choice remains to her now but to break off all relations with Hamlet. But what if they have already consummated their love? What if he has already sworn to her that he loves her and would never forsake her? Whom should she believe? Though Shakespeare tells us nothing to help us see into her heart, the actress playing Ophelia must know what she feels about Hamlet. Most critics agree that Ophelia and Hamlet have already been intimate, that Ophelia is deeply smitten with true love for the Prince, and that her father and brother's words hurt her deeply. Were this conjecture not true, Ophelia's motivation for her subsequent actions would be questionable.

Glossary

convoy is assistant a means of conveyance is available.

toy in blood trifling youthful passion.

primy in its prime, youthful.

suppliance of a minute a minute's pastime.

crescent increasing, growing.

temple body; the temple of the soul.

cautel craft, deceit.

will desire.

his greatness weigh'd considering his high position.

carve choose.

credent credulous.

chaste treasure precious chastity.

unmaster'd importunity uncontrolled and determined wooing.

chariest most modest and virtuous.

prodigal exceedingly or recklessly wasteful, spendthrift.

buttons buds.

contagious blastments destructive blights.

recks not his own rede doesn't take his own advice.

fear me not don't be afraid for me.

character a pun on character in the sense of personal qualities.

unproportion'd overly emotional, excessive.

adoption tried friendship that has stood the test of time.

unfledg'd immature (literally designating a young bird without feathers and thus not able to fly).

censure opinion

husbandry thrift.

season ripen.

tend attend, wait.

Marry a Common Elizabethan expletive for Mary, referring to the Virgin Mary.

put on me reported to me.

sterling true currency (with the value of an English silver penny).

crack the wind of overwork. The phrase comes from working a horse so hard that it becomes winded.

springes snares consisting of a noose attached to something under tension, as a bent tree branch.

woodcocks birds thought of as being stupid because they are easily caught; hence, a person who is a fool or a dupe.

brokers people who act as agents or intermediaries in negotiating contracts, buying and selling, and so forth.

investments garments.

this is for all to sum up.

Act I
Scene 4

Summary

In accordance with their plan, Horatio and Marcellus meet Hamlet on the battlements of the castle. A trumpet sounds, and the Prince bitterly comments on the King's propensity for wine and revelry. He disapproves of this behavior as it reflects badly on all Danes and gives them a reputation for drunkenness that makes them the butt of jokes. He points out that people often judge a man of great stature by his smallest "mole of nature" and not by his strength. Before the discussion can go further, Horatio notices the Ghost's arrival.

Despite his uncertainty as to whether the Ghost "airs from heaven or blasts from hell," or whether the Ghost harbors "wicked or charitable" intentions, Hamlet immediately identifies the apparition as his father. He empowers the Ghost to explain the purpose of his visit and charges the spirit to speak and make things clear. The Ghost beckons Hamlet to follow, and, despite the entreaties of his comrades to beware, Hamlet follows the spirit into the night.

Commentary

Again Hamlet reveals his preoccupation with the disparity between appearance and reality. Claudius appears to be a powerful man, yet harbors a decided weakness for wine and revelry. Thus, says Hamlet, Claudius makes all Danes seem drunkards to their critics and attracts disrespect from both allies and enemies. Just as an individual's weaknesses can overshadow all virtue, so one "swinish" man, especially a swinish leader, can overshadow all virtuous compatriots. Hamlet completes his critique of the new king/satyr the very moment before the old king, the great Hyperion himself, appears. Claudius' evil habits garner more suspicions than the Ghost's motives. The true evil lies in the heart of the successor, and the degeneracy of the court reflects the necessary outcome of foul deeds.

Hamlet's speech about Claudius' carousing is important on a number of levels. Critics refer to this speech as the "dram of evil" speech because Hamlet ends it by saying, "The dram of evil / Doth all the noble substance of a doubt, / To his own scandal." In this speech, Hamlet indicts the Danish people, including himself—he is, after all, "to the manner born"—for their hedonism. Large appetites for wine and revelry indicate the kind of dissipation that weakens cultures and usurps nations. The fact that "swinish" behavior characterizes the Danish collective reputation embarrasses Hamlet.

Critics have viewed *Hamlet* as a latter-day morality play in which Hamlet, a sort of Renaissance Everyman, must navigate through moral depravity toward the light of reason and good deeds to find his way to righteousness. His sense of honor drives him to do the right thing, but the right thing actually contradicts God's law. Hamlet is torn between right and right rather than right and wrong. Hamlet's definition of the subjective "right" differs drastically from Claudius' definition. As A.C. Bradley points out, Hamlet cares for nothing so much as he cares for "human worth," and Hamlet has an "aversion to evil." In fact, Bradley suggests that we might consider the play a "tragedy of moral idealism as much as a tragedy of reflection."

Glossary

shrewdly bitterly.

rouse a toast in which all glasses must be drained before lowering.

wassail revelry, carousing.

Up-spring a high-kicking, wild German dance.

Rhenish Rhine wine.

bray out celebrate.

the triumph of his pledge his drinking ability.

to the manner born accustomed to it since a child.

traduc'd and tax'd defamed and censored.

of by.

clepe to call or address (a person).

mole blemish.

o'er-leavens ferments.

nature's livery, or fortune's star inborn or the result of bad luck.

His virtues else his other virtues.

general censure public's judgment.

The dram of evil / Doth all the noble substance of a doubt, / To his own scandal a much-disputed passage. Perhaps a line is missing. The general meaning seems to be that it takes only a small portion of evil to bring a scandal on the entire substance, however noble it may otherwise be.

spirit of health There are two possible meanings. First, a saved (healthy) soul, not a lost one. Second, a healing or beneficent spirit.

goblin damn'd damned agent of the devil. Hamlet, from the very first, seems to question the authenticity of the ghost as the true spirit of his father.

hearsed buried.

cerements cloths or sheets wrapped around a dead person; shrouds.

inurn'd buried; entombed (literally, put the ashes of a dead person into an urn).

complete steel full armor.

flood sea. Elsinore is situated on the Danish coast.

beetles o'er overhangs.

toys of desperation desperate fancies or impulses—referring to the impulse to jump off a high place.

Nemean in Greek mythology, a reference to a fierce lion from Nemea killed by Hercules as the first of his twelve labors.

lets hinders.

Act I
Scene 5

Summary

Back on the parapet—the outer walls of Castle Elsinore—Hamlet follows the Ghost, who admits that he is the spirit of King Hamlet and tells his son to hear him out. His time is short before he must return to Purgatory. He cannot share any of the secrets of life in purgatory, but he has a tale of woe he desperately needs to pass on to his son. Before he will give Hamlet any details, however, he charges the Prince to avenge his murder. The words of the Ghost horrify Hamlet, for they confirm his fears. Hurrying because he can "scent the morning," King Hamlet tells his son that Claudius seduced his seemingly virtuous queen, and then crept to where his brother lay napping and poured a lethal poison in King Hamlet's ear. The poison quickly curdled King Hamlet's blood, robbing him of both his life and the opportunity for absolution.

The Ghost tells Hamlet to "Remember me," but only after he instructs him to leave Gertrude alone. So Hamlet must wrest retribution only from Claudius. The Ghost exits, leaving Hamlet incensed. Hamlet answers the worried calls of Horatio and Marcellus, telling them nothing specific but demanding that they both take an oath to tell no one what they have seen and heard. In confidence, Hamlet tells Horatio that he will pretend to be mad so that he may spy on his mother and uncle. After Horatio has sworn allegiance, Hamlet bids the departed Ghost to rest and then curses his fate before exiting with the other men.

Commentary

King Hamlet's Ghost introduces himself in a way that most certainly evoked the sympathy of the Elizabethan audience. He tells Hamlet that his brother robbed him of everything he was, all that he owned, including his everlasting soul. In the same way that the Bible engenders sympathy for Abel and condemns Cain for the fratricide, Shakespeare favors the murdered brother.

Hamlet is quick to believe the Ghost because the spirit's words confirm his worst fear: Claudius murdered King Hamlet. For the

Elizabethan/Jacobean audience who attended the first performances of *Hamlet,* murder of a king was in itself cause for alarm. Consider that the English people believed that their monarchs ruled by Divine Right, that God Himself appointed them to rule the land. The Church of England went so far as to attribute to the monarch the highest order of executive power in the church as well. In all ways, the English monarch represented God on earth. King Hamlet's murder makes the Ghost a most sympathetic figure to Shakespeare's audiences. No one would have questioned the existence of that Ghost, and few would have believed—even for a moment, as Hamlet does—that the Ghost could be a devil.

The fact that his mother's lover is also her husband's murderer exacerbates Gertrude's crime of incest. Hamlet is bereft of choice. He may have an aversion to violence, and he may live by strict Christian principles, but he must avenge his father's honor. Hamlet sees no way to honor his father except by killing Claudius. Doubly impelled by his father's orders and by tradition, Hamlet becomes a prisoner of his obligation for revenge.

The major conflict here is obvious. Christianity negated the Hebraic notion of "an eye for an eye"; the notion seemed barbaric to the Renaissance population. Further, the medieval custom of a blood feud wherein the closest relative of a murdered man must avenge the death had become passé. Society more often supported the notion of mercy and forgiveness, concepts Shakespeare explored in an earlier play, *Merchant of Venice.* In *Merchant,* the audience despises the antagonist precisely because he insists on a blood feud. In *Hamlet,* Shakespeare asks the audience to empathize with Hamlet's desire for redress. Hamlet is a sympathetic character precisely because the notion of revenge drives him while his Christian morality and inclination simultaneously exhort him to be charitable.

The major issues of the play are now out in the open and conjoined: By marrying Claudius, Gertrude has committed incest and has failed to carry out her duties to her slain husband. In Claudius, because of his duplicity, these sins are unforgivable. How his people perceive him concerns Claudius more than making things right with Hamlet, Gertrude, or the people of Denmark. On the other hand, Gertrude is a woman who has been led by her weakness and frailty to follow the charismatic devil of a king to his bed.

Hamlet swears Horatio and Marcellus to secrecy and garners further support from his audience. His genuine leadership capability and honest friendship for Horatio inspire great loyalty from the two men, and that loyalty is clearly Hamlet's earned reward for his strength of character.

Hamlet tells Horatio that he plans to feign madness before the King and the court. The madness will render him invisible so that he might observe and discern the best way and time for his revenge. Hamlet's meaning here remains ambiguous. Is his madness a mask? A costume? A lie? The answer to this question provides the key to Hamlet's characterization, and an actor playing the role must decide what that "putting on" signifies. In some portrayals, Hamlet pretends to be mad; in others, while he may believe he is pretending, he is quite mad. In still others, Hamlet's madness grows as he develops. In others again, Hamlet is a child who can't grow up and accept the burdens of adulthood, which include his duties to his slain father. Shakespeare seems to have deliberately left Hamlet's ruse ambiguous enough so that the performances of the role may vary.

Glossary

Unhouseled, disappointed, unaneled without the sacraments of communion, penance, and extreme unction.

Hic et ubique Latin for here and everywhere.

truepenny honest fellow.

knotted and combined locks hair lying together in a mass.

porpentine porcupine.

Act II
Scene 1

Summary

Polonius meets with his sly servant Reynaldo and tells him to go to Paris and spy on Laertes. He charges the servant to find any Danes living in Paris and to question them as to Laertes' whereabouts and reputation. Polonius even goes so far as to give Reynaldo permission to use lies to entrap Laertes. After Reynaldo exits in pursuit of his mission, Ophelia enters and tells Polonius that she has been horrified by the Prince. Hamlet came to her in her sewing room with his jacket askew and unfastened, and wearing no hat; his stockings were filthy and unfastened, drooping at his ankles; and he was pale and trembling, looking "piteous." Polonius diagnoses Hamlet's condition as madness due to his love of Ophelia, brought about because Ophelia obeyed her father and spurned Hamlet's advances. Polonius decides to take his information to the King.

Commentary

Many critics, including T.S. Eliot, believe this scene is irrelevant to the play. However, the scene actually mirrors themes that are central to the play's purpose. Appearance and reality are disparate entities that contradict one another.

In Act II, Scene 1, the apparently caring, nurturing father Polonius hires the shady Reynaldo (The Fox) to spy on Laertes. Polonius tells Reynaldo that he suspects the worst of Laertes and wants reports of all his dirtiest deeds gleaned from the most deceptive spying. He tells Reynaldo to look into Laertes' life in Paris even if he needs to accuse his son falsely—'What forgeries you please.'" Polonius will pay Reynaldo to discredit Laertes with negative reports—both real and imagined—in order to teach his son the importance of reputation. The duplicity of this encounter foreshadows the behavior that will characterize Polonius throughout the play.

In the second part of the scene, Ophelia enters and reports that Hamlet has been acting incomprehensibly. She describes with painter's language the way Hamlet is attired:

> Lord Hamlet with his doublet unbraced
> No hat upon his head, his stockings fouled,
> Ungartered, and down-gyved to his ankle
> Pale as his shirt, his knees knocking each other,
> And with a look so piteous in purport
> As if he had been loosèd out of hell
> To speak of horrors—he comes before me.

The description is one that Polonius immediately recognizes—"Mad for thy love?"—because Hamlet's appearance embodies the contemporary stereotype of the spurned lover, indicating that his main objective in visiting Ophelia is to use Ophelia to convince others that his insanity was not due to any mysterious unknown cause, but to this disappointment, and so to allay the suspicions of the King. Thus, Ophelia's purpose in this scene seems to be to give credence to the notion that Hamlet never loved Ophelia at all, but merely used her. If so, then Hamlet is as guilty of deceptiveness as are those he judges.

Glossary

Danskers Danes.

what means what their income is.

keep lodge.

drabbing associating with prostitutes.

season qualify.

incontinency without self-restraint, especially in regard to sexual activity.

quaintly skillfully, ingeniously.

unreclaimed untamed.

of general assault common to all men.

videlicet (Latin) that is; namely.

windlasses roundabout means.

assays of bias This is a metaphor from the game of lawn bowling; the weight in the ball, which causes it to follow a curved line, is called the bias. Hence the meaning of the phrase is "indirect attempts."

doublet a man's close-fitting jacket, with or without sleeves, worn chiefly from the 14th to the 16th centuries. The coat that was fastened (braced) to the hose (short breeches) by laces. When a man was relaxing or careless of appearance, he "unbrac'd," much like a man today loosens his tie or takes off his suit jacket.

down gyved fallen, like fetters, about his ankles.

ecstasy madness

fordoes destroys.

jealousy suspicion.

cast beyond ourselves look beyond what we know or understand.

Act II
Scene 2

Summary

The King and Queen enter with Rosencrantz and Guildenstern and others. King Claudius has summoned Hamlet's two school chums to Elsinore to have them spy on the Prince and report back to Claudius, recounting Hamlet's every move. The Queen promises them handsome compensation for their spying and assures them that Hamlet's own good requires the service. Rosencrantz and Guildenstern agree. The two leave to seek Prince Hamlet, and the King and Queen turn their attention to Polonius, who claims to have the answer to Prince Hamlet's affliction. He promises to elaborate further after Claudius receives his newly arrived ambassadors from Norway.

When Polonius exits, Gertrude scoffs at the old man's intimations. She remains certain that Hamlet's woes are caused by the old king's death and her hasty remarriage. Polonius returns with Ambassadors Voltemand and Cornelius. They bring news from Norway that the old and ailing king, brother to the slain King Fortinbras, has managed to restrain his nephew, young Fortinbras, from invading Denmark. In return, however, the old man asks that Denmark provide some assistance in Fortinbras' campaign against Poland—that Claudius allow Fortinbras to pass through Denmark on his way to Poland.

As soon as the ambassadors leave, Polonius launches into an elaborate discussion on the meaning of life and duty, promising to be brief and then launching into further wordiness. Finally, Polonius asserts that Hamlet is mad. Having no patience for Polonius, Gertrude admonishes him. Again promising to be less loquacious, Polonius makes showy, wavy motions with his arms and then reads a letter he confiscated from his daughter, written in the Prince's hand. Polonius criticizes the highly dramatic, artificial prose with random rhymes in which Hamlet has written the note and tells Claudius and Gertrude that he has forbidden Ophelia to accept any advances from the Prince. That is the order, Polonius claims, that has led poor Hamlet into madness.

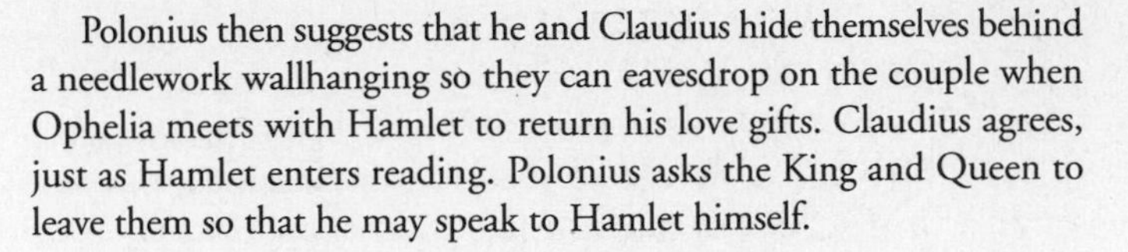

Polonius then suggests that he and Claudius hide themselves behind a needlework wallhanging so they can eavesdrop on the couple when Ophelia meets with Hamlet to return his love gifts. Claudius agrees, just as Hamlet enters reading. Polonius asks the King and Queen to leave them so that he may speak to Hamlet himself.

In the encounter that follows between Hamlet and Polonius, Hamlet warns Polonius to watch his daughter carefully and then toys with Polonius' limited wit. The exchange convinces Polonius that Hamlet is lovesick when, in actuality, Hamlet's responses have done little but ridicule Polonius. Polonius leaves, and Rosencrantz and Guildenstern enter. Hamlet greets them as his "excellent good friends" and asks why they have come to his prison. They grouse at his choice of words, but he tells them, "Denmark's a prison." Rosencrantz wittily replies, "Then is the world one." Hamlet breaks through his friends' resistance, and the two finally admit that the King and Queen sent them to observe Hamlet and provide them with details of his behavior. Hamlet's melancholy then erupts in a blank verse complaint that he has lately "lost all my mirth." He laments that a foul and sickening fog now besmirches the heavens, which he once saw as a canopy "fretted with golden fire." Hamlet then indicts the very nature of mankind.

Rosencrantz seizes the opportunity to announce the arrival of the players, and Hamlet's mood shifts yet again. Ecstatic at the opportunity for diversion, Hamlet asks who the players are and why they are on the road. Rosencrantz answers that they are on the road because a company of child actors has usurped the London stage. Hamlet responds by saying that he welcomes Rosencrantz and Guildenstern as he welcomes the actors and hopes he can be a worthy host. Polonius enters to announce the arrival of the players.

When the players enter, Hamlet requests that the lead player perform a speech from Virgil's *Aeneid* in which Aeneas tells Queen Dido the story of Phyrrus, whose father Achilles was killed at Rome. The player performs the speech and moves himself to tears over Hecuba's horror at seeing her husband dismembered. Hamlet asks Polonius to see to the players' lodging, and, as soon as the Lord Chamberlain has left, he tells the small group of players remaining on-stage his plans for their performance of *The Murder of Gonzago.* He tells them that he will provide them with twelve to sixteen original lines that he wants them to add to the play. They agree, and they leave.

Hamlet then reveals his real intentions for *The Murder of Gonzago.* The players will perform the play with an enhanced scene, which will enact the murder the Ghost has described. Hamlet hopes that seeing his crime reenacted in front of the assembled audience will make Claudius act guilty and reveal that he murdered King Hamlet. Such an admission will prove to Hamlet, once and for all, that the Ghost is real and not simply a devil or the figment of his imagination.

Commentary

Gertrude implies in her opening words to Rosencrantz and Guildenstern that the she and Claudius have invited the pair to Denmark for Hamlet's benefit. Although Claudius may have ulterior motives, Gertrude is the person who insisted on contacting Rosencrantz and Guildenstern and bringing them to court because of the friendship and respect that Hamlet bears for them. At this point in the play, one can reasonably assume that both Claudius and Gertrude had Hamlet's welfare in mind when they summoned the two Germans to court.

Claudius, however, is once again aware that all eyes are on him as he solicitously welcomes Rosencrantz and Guildenstern and expresses his grave concern for "Hamlet's transformation." Although Shakespeare gives no suggestion that Claudius had anything but Hamlet's welfare in mind when he summoned Rosencrantz and Guildenstern to court, the audience knows that Claudius does nothing without self-promotion in mind. His suggestion that they report back any affliction of Hamlet's echoes Polonius' instructions to Reynaldo in Scene 1 regarding Laertes. Both Polonius and Claudius exhibit distrust and deception when dealing with their heirs. When Rosencrantz and Guildenstern heartily agree to do the King's and Queen's bidding, Gertrude promises they will receive "such thanks / As fits a king's remembrance." Claudius has successfully deceived Gertrude as well, convincing her that he loves Prince Hamlet.

When Polonius ushers in Cornelius and Voltemand—Claudius' ambassadors to Norway—the old man entices the King with a promise that he knows something about the Lord Hamlet that Gertrude and Claudius cannot know. He refuses to divulge any information until after the ambassadors have left, but he creates excitement over his "find." Gertrude, motivated only by her deep, even overprotective, love for her son, remains skeptical about Polonius' ability to help.

The ambassadors bring good news for Claudius, which cheers the King, and he plans a celebratory party. Shakespeare presents here another mirror. Young Fortinbras, a dutiful nephew whose uncle has ascended to the throne that might have been his, obeys his uncle/sovreign's request to show Denmark leniency. Claudius knows of no reason that his nephew/subject would be less cooperative or less charitable, and he is more than willing to toy with Hamlet's good nature.

Character Insight

Gertrude expresses her concern for and sensitivity toward Hamlet. She fully understands the trauma he has experienced in returning to Denmark to find his world shattered and reordered. Polonius' plan to spy on Hamlet, to trap him, as it were, by exposing a private letter the old man has impounded from his daughter, does not please Gertrude. Her son's welfare concerns her far more than affairs of state. However, Gertrude agrees to Polonius' plan because it affords her the hope that Hamlet's madness merely results from unrequited love, which can be easily remedied. The old man clearly agitates Gertrude, who urges him to disclose something substantive: "More matter and less art." However, Polonius' report finally wins her over, and she agrees to Polonius' plan to spy on Hamlet. Another deception is premeditated and prearranged, another of Polonius' "springes to catch woodcocks."

That both Gertrude and Ophelia are complicit with the entrapment is a key to Hamlet's distrust of women and of his inability to allow himself to love either of them. Hamlet enters in his state of apparent madness. Yet, mad with despair as he may seem on the surface, Hamlet remains sharp enough to volley artfully with words that confound Polonius' limited wit. Hamlet calls the old man a fishmonger, a term rife with double entendre. Because "fish" was an off-color allusion to women, "fish sellers" were those who sold women's favors—in other words, pimps.

Hamlet demonstrates his acute sense of wordplay with his sad cynicism on the subject of honesty. "To be honest, as this world goes, is to be one man picked in ten thousand." But he clearly convinces Polonius that he is not rational. "How pregnant sometimes his replies are! A happiness that often madness hits on, which reason and sanity could not so prosperously be delivered of." Then again, as soon as Polonius exits, Hamlet reveals his true level of reason: "These tedious fools." He understands that Polonius is not the only old man he needs to worry about.

Rosencrantz and Guildenstern return, and Hamlet elucidates his astuteness once more. He manipulates his "excellent good friends" into admitting they have been sent for. He calls fortune a whore, suggesting that one can buy luck and fate . . . like friendship. He proves that he understands the duplicitous nature of their visit. He further clarifies his presence of mind through his lucid discourse on the nature of dreams and the paradox of human existence.

Prison imagery surrounds this scene. "Denmark's a prison," he says. In answer to Rosencrantz's retort that "then the world must be one," Hamlet assents but asserts that Denmark is "One o' the worst." The brooding clarity with which Hamlet perceives his predicament reminds us that he has announced that he will wear an antic disposition—that he is faking his madness.

When Polonius announces the arrival of the players and Hamlet again plays with what he perceives as Polonius' meager intelligence, however, Polonius again concludes that Ophelia's rejection is the cause of Hamlet's madness.

After the player's rendition of Hecuba's horror, Hamlet expounds to himself on the crux of his dilemma. He compares himself to an actor playing out the drama of his own life, but he cannot find the motivation to move beyond his immobilized state of melancholy. He is stuck in words, in the idea of action, terrified to move forward. The actor playacting as Phyrrus, a fictional character, is moved to kill his father's killer; the actor relating a fairytale about a woman's woes is capable of real emotion. Hamlet is an actor prompted by heaven and hell to seek revenge for his murdered father but is unschooled in his art and hesitates for fear of the consequences. His judgmental conscience stifles his emotions. He cannot sympathize with Gertrude or follow the Ghost's instructions to defend her honor because his fears blind him. His incessant pandering to words emasculates him. "That I . . . must, like a whore, unpack my heart with words." But because he is a man of words, he uses first the words of the play in his plan to strike at the king.

Hamlet ends the scene by revealing his plan to entrap the King by manipulating the play to force the King's conscience to incriminate him. This time the premeditated duplicity belongs to Hamlet. Surrounded by false friends and dubious love, Hamlet recognizes an opportunity to use the honest deception of the stage to illuminate the truth.

Glossary

Sith since.

humour behavior.

from occasion by chance.

gentry courtesy.

supply and profit for the fulfillment and profitable conclusion of our hope.

in the full bent completely. Like a bow that is bent as far as it can be bent.

grace to bring honor to, dignify; with a pun on the prayer before meals.

in fine in the end.

assay of arms try to raise.

Perpend ponder.

more above moreover.

fell out occurred.

fain wish.

with sight with an indifferent eye.

round Polonius really means straight, but it is his nature to speak indirectly.

out of thy star beyond your station in life. Stars were believed to govern men's lives.

took the fruits of followed.

watch sleeplessness.

fishmonger a dealer in fish, or someone who sells women.

outstretched aspiring.

fay faith, used in oaths (by my *fay*!); with a pun on fairy.

fretted having an ornamental pattern of small, straight bars intersecting or joining one another, usually at right angles, to form a regular design, as for a border or in an architectural relief; decorated like the painted ceiling over the stage at The Globe.

coted overtook.

foil and target fencing rapier and small shield.

Humorous Man the player of character parts.

tickle sere made to laugh easily.

half limp.

aery nest.

eyases unfledged birds, especially young hawks taken from the nest for training in falconry.

berattle abuse.

escoted paid.

tarre urge.

mows grimaces (twistings or distortions of the face).

Roscius the most famous of ancient Roman actors.

Buz, buz a slang expression for "tell me something I don't know."

scene individable preserving the unities.

poem unlimited a play that observed none of the ancient rules.

Seneca (*c.* 4? B.C.3A.D. 65); Roman philosopher, dramatist, and statesman.

Plautus (254?-184 B.C.); Roman writer of comic dramas.

law of writ classical plays.

liberty modern plays.

Jephthah a judge in the Bible who sacrificed his daughter in fulfillment of a vow (Judg. 11:30-40).

valanced bearded.

chopine a woman's shoe with a very thick sole, as of cork.

digested organized.

sallets tasty bits.

"Twas Aeneas' tale to Dido" the story of the sack of Troy as told to Queen Dido by Aeneas. (Virgil's *Aeneid* contains the story.)

Priam legendary king of Troy, who reigned during the Trojan War; he was the father of Hector and Paris.

Pyrrhus in Greek mythology, the son of Achilles; one of the Greeks concealed in the famous wooden horse.

Hyrcanian beast tiger from Hyrcania, mentioned in the Aeneid.

total gules completely red.

impasted made into a paste (the slain, not Pyrrhus).

carbuncles precious stones of fiery red color.

Ilium Latin name for Troy

rack cloud formations, a broken mass of clouds blown by the wind.

orb the earth.

Cyclops in Greek mythology, any of a race of giants who have only one eye, in the middle of the forehead; they assisted Vulcan, the god of fire.

proof eterne everlasting protection.

fellies the segments forming the rim of a spoked wheel.

nave rim; the hub of a wheel.

Hecuba in Homer's *Iliad*, the wife of Priam and mother of Hector, Troilus, Paris, and Cassandra.

mobled wearing ruffled collars popular in Elizabethan England.

bisson rheum blinding tears.

clout a piece of cloth; a rag.

milch milky, moist.

muddy-mettled dull-spirited.

peak mope.

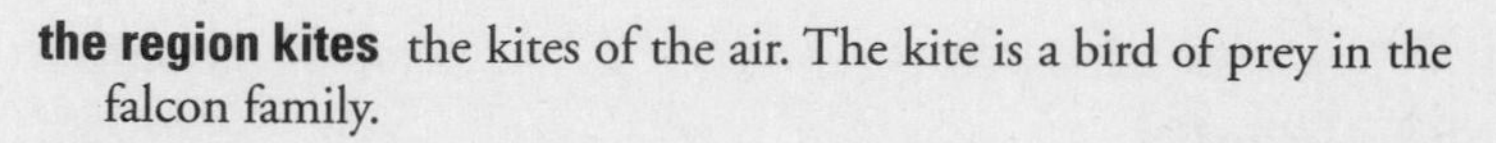

the region kites the kites of the air. The kite is a bird of prey in the falcon family.

this slave's offal the entrails of a butchered animal; here, the king's guts.

scullion a servant doing the rough, dirty work in a kitchen.

blench to shrink back, as in fear; flinch.

Act III
Scene 1

Summary

The King and Queen enter with Rosencrantz, Guildenstern, Polonius, Ophelia, and members of the court. Claudius questions Rosencrantz and Guildenstern about Hamlet's madness, asking if they have found a reason for Hamlet's behavior. Rosencrantz answers that the Prince has admitted to being distracted but will not say from what. Guildenstern says that Hamlet has been crafty in disguising his motivations. The two report that Hamlet is very excited about the play to be presented, and Claudius asks them to encourage him in this regard. Rosencrantz and Guildenstern leave.

Claudius orders Gertrude to leave so that he and Polonius can spy on Hamlet, who has an imminent meeting with Ophelia. Ophelia enters, and the Queen, in a moment of maternal affection, tells Ophelia that she hopes that Hamlet and Ophelia will patch up their broken romance so that Hamlet can get on with his life. Gertrude exits. Polonius greets Ophelia and instructs her to pretend to read a book so that her being alone will not seem unusual to Hamlet. Ophelia complies and waits with a book while the two men hide. Hamlet enters, speaking his "To be or not to be" soliloquy. He ponders the nature of being and nothingness, and then notices Ophelia reading. Hamlet, assuming that she is reading prayers, asks her to pray for him. She tells him she wishes to return to him gifts he has given her. He responds that he has given her no gifts. She insists that he did give her gifts, and she claims that he gave the gifts to her with words that made them seem symbols of great love. Again he denies having given her the gifts at all and further denies having ever loved her. He questions her honesty and, in response to her bewilderment, tells her that all men are untrustworthy knaves and that she would be better off in a nunnery.

To Ophelia's further consternation, Hamlet then abruptly demands that she disclose the current whereabouts of her father. She lies and says that he is at home. Enraged, Hamlet curses her, predicting a disaster for her dowry. He tells her again to go to a nunnery. As Ophelia frets over his apparently fled sanity, he says that he knows that women are two faced and cannot be trusted; they all deserve to be cast aside. Then he leaves.

Left alone, Ophelia bemoans what she considers to be Hamlet's descent into complete insanity. Claudius and Polonius join her and assess what they have overheard and seen. The King doubts that love has ruined Hamlet's mind; he tells Polonius that he will send Hamlet to England. Polonius, still convinced that love afflicts Hamlet, urges Claudius to make one more attempt to ferret out a satisfying reason for Hamlet's behavior. He tells the King to send Hamlet to Gertrude's quarters later that evening. There, while Polonius hides behind the arras, Gertrude should attempt to cajole Hamlet into revealing his innermost thoughts with Polonius as witness. Claudius agrees.

Commentary

Claudius' entrance speech reveals two very significant aspects of his character: (1) that he is aware of the growing threat Hamlet poses for him, and (2) that he is absolutely in control and capable of decisive action. He provides a stark contrast to Hamlet, who becomes entirely incapacitated by the very idea of action. The more Claudius knows, the more he calculates and acts; the more Hamlet knows, the more he thinks and bandies words. Hamlet's "turbulent lunacy" places them both in danger.

The characters enact two more premeditated entrapments. First, Claudius sends Rosencrantz and Guildenstern to continue their spying. Second, Polonius and Claudius hatch their plot to have Ophelia stage a confrontation in which Hamlet will reveal himself to Ophelia while Claudius and Polonius spy.

Claudius appears to care deeply about his tortured nephew but confesses his guilty conscience in an aside. Claudius gradually reveals the depth of his criminality and at the same time engenders sympathy—the paradox of evil—by exposing his human fallibility. He sees his guilt in Polonius' charge that they could sugarcoat the devil. "Oh, 'tis too true," says Claudius. "How smart a lash that speech doth give my conscience!" Even a whore can look innocent when painted, and so his ugly deed looks honorable when clouded by pretty words. Still he feels the weight of his sin. Claudius presents a formidable foe for Hamlet. Both men have now revealed their cunning and sensitive comprehension of

the human condition. They are evenly matched except that Claudius has the advantage of political power— for the moment.

In this scene, Gertrude remains as the Ghost had described her, the loving mother caught in Claudius' web. She asks Rosencrantz and Guildenstern whether they've tried to amuse her melancholy son, and she tells Ophelia she truly hopes the young woman's virtues can bring Hamlet back to his senses. Ophelia doesn't answer the Queen, and the audience can only surmise that Gertrude has added fuel to the fire of the young girl's consternation.

Hamlet enters, brooding "To be or not to be." In *The Story of English,* Robert MacNeil writes, "When Hamlet says 'To be or not to be: that is the question,' he has summarized in one sentence all that follows." Many scholars consider this speech to be one of several existential manifestos in *Hamlet.* (Existentialism professes that the past and future are intangible; the present is all that humans can be sure of. For humans, being—what IS— is the only truth; everything else is nothing.)

In this soliloquy, Hamlet explores the ideas of being and nothingness by asserting a basic premise: We are born, we live, and we die. Because no one has returned from death to report, we remain ignorant of what death portends. Hence, Hamlet's dilemma encapsulates several universal human questions: Do we try to affect our fate? Do we take action in the face of great sorrow, or do we merely wallow in the suffering? Can we end our troubles by opposing them? How do we know? What is the nature of death? Do we sleep in death, or do we cease to sleep, thereby finding no rest at all?

Hamlet hopes that death is nothingness, that death will "end the heartache and the thousand natural shocks that flesh is heir to," that death will end thinking, knowing, and remembering. But he fears that, in death, he will be haunted interminably by bad dreams of life itself, by dreams heavy with the memory of fear and pain. Ultimately, he says, that's why humans dread death. We fear that our consciences will torment us forever. Thus, human beings choose life, with its torment and burdens, chiefly to avoid death, the great unknown. However, death is, like life, inescapable, and Hamlet curses his luck for having been born at all.

Hamlet's dilemma underlies the entire soliloquy. If he kills Claudius, he will assuredly be killed himself. Hamlet is not sure he is ready for death; life is all he knows, and he fears the unknown. Further, he is not yet ready to take responsiblity for sending another human being into the throes of death. He understands his duty to avenge the murder that is now disclosed, and he accepts responsibility for the Ghost's torment, but he knows that by killing Claudius he could be consigning himself to his father's fate for all eternity. Hamlet ends his revery when he sees Ophelia enter, engrossed in her book. He entreats her to remember him in her prayers. His words startle her, and she responds by inquiring after his health. Immediately, she recovers and launches into her assigned speech:

> My lord, I have remembrances of yours
> That I have longèd long to redeliver.
> I pray you now receive them.

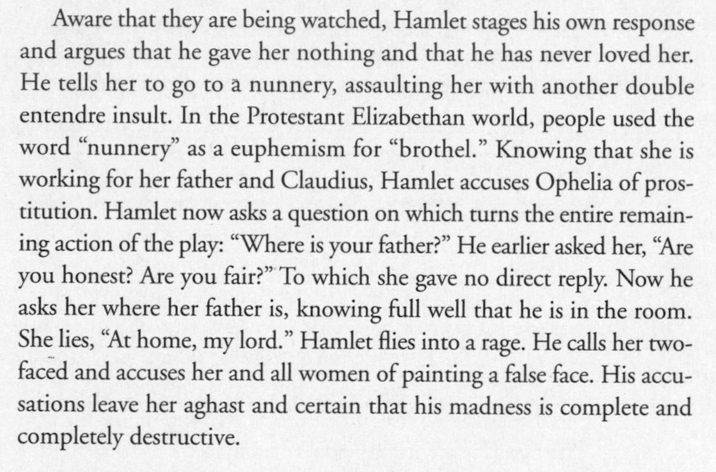

Aware that they are being watched, Hamlet stages his own response and argues that he gave her nothing and that he has never loved her. He tells her to go to a nunnery, assaulting her with another double entendre insult. In the Protestant Elizabethan world, people used the word "nunnery" as a euphemism for "brothel." Knowing that she is working for her father and Claudius, Hamlet accuses Ophelia of prostitution. Hamlet now asks a question on which turns the entire remaining action of the play: "Where is your father?" He earlier asked her, "Are you honest? Are you fair?" To which she gave no direct reply. Now he asks her where her father is, knowing full well that he is in the room. She lies, "At home, my lord." Hamlet flies into a rage. He calls her two-faced and accuses her and all women of painting a false face. His accusations leave her aghast and certain that his madness is complete and completely destructive.

Ophelia's response to Hamlet's question serves as the force that propels Hamlet's story to its tragic ends. If Ophelia had answered truthfully, if she had disclosed her father's whereabouts, if she had allied herself with Hamlet rather than with Claudius, if she had truly believed in her love for Hamlet, Ophelia might have saved Hamlet from his burden. The play could have been a romance rather than a tragedy. However, by confirming his belief in women's basic dishonesty—"frailty thy name is woman"—Ophelia seals her fate and Hamlet's at the same time.

Claudius and Polonius emerge from hiding, astounded. Claudius still finds Polonius' case for Hamlet's love of Ophelia dubious. Furthermore, Claudius questions Hamlet's madness. A master of deception, Claudius suspects that Hamlet is not as he seems and, as such, is a danger. He hatches his plan to exile the Prince to England. Perhaps to save Hamlet or perhaps to buy favor with the Queen, Polonius suggests yet another trap. Send Hamlet to see Gertrude, and instruct her to beg Hamlet to leave well enough alone. Polonius will spy as Hamlet confides in his mother. The old man expects that Hamlet will confess his love for Ophelia. For reasons he does not disclose, Claudius agrees to the plan. Hamlet knows that his elders are ganging up on him. He is furious and skittish, and his judgment is entirely impaired. Polonius' plot cannot help but backfire.

Glossary

drift of conference roundabout methods.

lawful espials spies who are justified in their action.

rub an obstacle hindrance, difficulty, or impediment.

contumely haughty and contemptuous rudeness; insulting and humiliating treatment or language.

bodkin a dagger or stiletto.

fardels burdens; misfortune.

bourn limit; boundary.

pitch and moment height and importance.

expectancy and rose bright hope (as future king).

mould of form pattern of manly beauty and behavior.

Act III
Scene 2

Summary

Hamlet meets with the actors and instructs them as to the nature of proper acting. He tells them not to overact, and not to use large gestures. He wishes them to be honest; he asks them to mirror nature, to be entirely realistic in their portrayals. Polonius enters and announces the arrival of the King and Queen to hear the play.

While the court assembles for the performance, Hamlet explains to Horatio how the play will help prove the Ghost's honesty and reveal Claudius' perfidy. He asks Horatio to watch the King and note his reaction to a specific speech in *Murder of Gonzago.* If the play does not reveal Claudius as the killer, Hamlet promises Horatio that he will admit to having seen a "damnèd ghost" rather than the honest spirit of his late father. Horatio, Hamlet's faithful friend, assures his Prince that he will follow Hamlet's instructions to the letter.

As the courtiers enter the hall, Claudius greets his nephew and asks how Hamlet is, and Hamlet gives a cryptic response. Then Hamlet and Polonius exchange a few words, and Polonius brags about having been murdered by Brutus when he played Julius Caesar in his student days. Hamlet derides Polonius, but Gertrude interrupts to invite her son to sit beside her. Hamlet chooses instead to lie down at Ophelia's feet. He converses a bit with Ophelia before the dumb show—a pantomime—begins, and she mistakes his manic behavior for merriness. The dumb show mimes the following: A man murders a king while he is sleeping in his garden, and his loving wife, initially inconsolable over the king's death, marries the usurper, who has crowned himself king.

When the dumb show ends, the players perform the actual play, which depicts the same plot as the pantomime. An intermission follows the Player Queen's declaration that she will never remarry should the Player King die. Hamlet seizes the moment to ask Gertrude what she thinks of the play, and Gertrude answers that she is enjoying the play but that the "Lady doth protest too much."

Claudius asks Hamlet for the play's title, to which Hamlet replies, *The Mousetrap.* He says that the play presents the true story of a murder carried out in Vienna. He explains the action of the play, and Ophelia congratulates Hamlet for his story-telling skill. Hamlet makes a crude pun, suggesting that he could interpret the actions of Ophelia and her lover if he could watch them. Ophelia accuses him of being keen (cruel), and Hamlet responds with another sexual innuendo. Hearing the word keen to mean sexually eager, he tells her she would have to work hard to relieve his sexual urges. Ophelia laughs that he is wittier than she, but more indecent. Hamlet says that women take their husbands for better or worse but then they deceive them.

As Lucianus, the Player King's nephew, pours poison in the ears of the sleeping Player King, Hamlet explains that the murderer will presently win the love of the dead Player King's widow. Claudius rises and calls for lights to be lit. Polonius repeats the order for the lights and stops the play. The King and his court exit, leaving Hamlet and Horatio to debrief. The two agree that the King's reaction implicates him in the murder of King Hamlet, and Hamlet says he is now convinced of the Ghost's trustworthiness.

Rosencrantz and Guildenstern enter and tell him that the King is displeased and the Queen wants Hamlet to join her in her quarters. Hamlet promises to obey. When a Player enters carrying a recorder, Hamlet seizes the opportunity to make an off-color allusion to Guildenstern's manhood and to chide him for being manipulative. Polonius enters and instructs Hamlet to visit his mother. Hamlet toys with Polonius, pretending to see shapes that do not exist, and then he asks that everyone leave him alone.

Hamlet observes that the dark time of night has come, when spirits and goblins rise from hell to spread their "Contagion to this world." Incensed by the hour and the events of the evening, Hamlet claims that he is ready to perform the task that duty demands—to "be cruel." First he will go to his mother and rebuke her, but he will not harm her. He then chides himself because his words are at war with his soul.

Commentary

Critics traditionally regard Scene 2 as more of a glimpse into Shakespeare's theatrical world than insight into *Hamlet.* Indeed, the first 50 lines do relate how Shakespeare interpreted an actor's job, and what he expected of his actors. We know that he advocated a natural style of acting rather than the declamatory style—a style of acting in which players use large gestures such as "sawing the air" and exaggerated motion in conjunction with consistently loud line readings. We also know that he advocated that actors take their direction from the script.

In addition to a primer on acting, however, Scene 2 reveals a great deal about Hamlet's psycho-emotional makeup. Still imprisoned by words and surrounded by staging, acting, and seeming, Hamlet now directs his own world, if only for a moment. Ensuring that the play be "as 't were the mirror up to nature" is critical so that Claudius will not miss seeing his own reflection in the Player King's murderous nephew. Were the actors to fail to "suit the actor to the word," were they "too tame" or too cruel, then Claudius might dismiss the tragedy as mere melodrama. The "whirlwind of passion" would negate true feeling, and Claudius' conscience would miss its examination.

Hamlet's instructions to the actors also serve to demonstrate how well Hamlet is prepared to play his role, to put on his antic disposition. Hamlet clearly possesses an actor's sensibility and understands that, in order to sell a performance an actor must become his role. This insight into Hamlet's psyche may provide one answer to the question that people most often raise concerning Hamlet's character: Is he truly mad, or is he truly acting? This scene confirms the possibility that Hamlet represents an actor who plays his role so well that he loses himself in the role and becomes what he pretends to be. What begins as an antic disposition becomes his hopeless, true self.

We can see Hamlet's instructions to the actors from a third angle as well. In his world of deception and betrayal, Hamlet recognizes the need to exercise reason and caution, and to remain aloof from blind passion. Thus he can again justify his inaction and validate his slow approach to avenging his father's murder. He must assure himself once more that this is his father's spirit and not a demon from hell. Hence, he informs Horatio of the plan so that he has a man who is "not passion's slave" to observe the King and confirm his reactions. Identifying the Ghost's validity is critical. Should it prove itself a demon, Hamlet's worst fears would be warranted, and Claudius may be blameless.

While waiting, Claudius asks after Hamlet's health, and Hamlet answers in seeming madness: "Excellent, i'faith, of the chameleon's dish: I eat the air, promise-crammed. You cannot feed capons so." Claudius is nearly speechless in response to Hamlet's answer. Hamlet has accused him of having emasculated (capons) and disinherited his nephew, and all he can say is, "I have nothing with this answer Hamlet, these words are not mine." He has all but said a childish, "Oh, shut up."

Polonius then diverts all attention with tales of his fleeting career as an actor playing Julius Caesar while at the university.

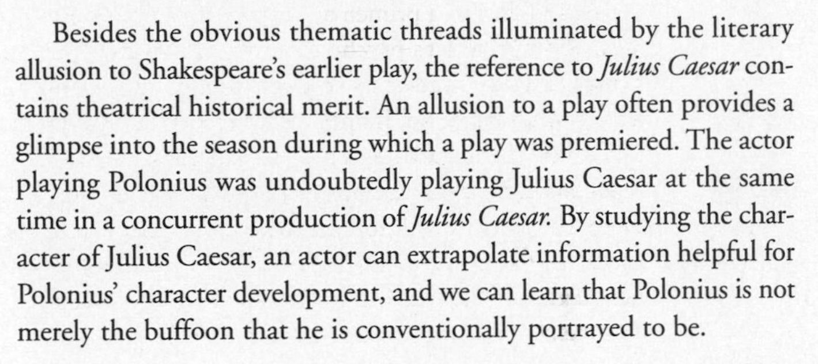

Besides the obvious thematic threads illuminated by the literary allusion to Shakespeare's earlier play, the reference to *Julius Caesar* contains theatrical historical merit. An allusion to a play often provides a glimpse into the season during which a play was premiered. The actor playing Polonius was undoubtedly playing Julius Caesar at the same time in a concurrent production of *Julius Caesar.* By studying the character of Julius Caesar, an actor can extrapolate information helpful for Polonius' character development, and we can learn that Polonius is not merely the buffoon that he is conventionally portrayed to be.

Hamlet sits by Ophelia and asks to put his head in her lap, a request that is demeaning in public while at the same time indicating that the two have a far more intimate relationship than has been indicated thus far. Ophelia seems pleased with his attention and says, "You are merry, my lord." Hamlet's cynicism reemerges, and he again casts aspersions at his mother. Once again he convinces everyone that he is mad.

Ophelia's question, "What means this, my lord?" reflects the fact that the guests did not expect a dumb show. Dumb shows no longer preceded tragedies by the time of *Hamlet's* first production, and Shakespeare's desire to include one baffles critics. Perhaps Shakespeare thought it clarified elements of the story that he needed in order to heighten the intensity of contrast between the play and the play within the play.

Whatever the reason for the dumb show, the actual speaking play follows, and Claudius remains unperturbed until the Player King actually pours the poison in his brother's ear. He then jumps up in a moment of heightened drama and, after his courtiers notice him, he shouts, "Give me some lights." The King has sprung Hamlet's *Mousetrap;* Claudius' own revulsion to *The Murder of Gonzago* catches him. Hamlet's mission now becomes obligatory. Not only does he know he must avenge his father's death, but Horatio also knows—and the entire court may now suspect foul play in the death of their former king, so that his inaction is unmanly. Hamlet must act decisively and immediately.

And yet, Hamlet keeps talking. He volleys words about his unlikely succession to Claudius' throne with Rosencrantz and Guildenstern. Finally he agrees to visit Gertrude. Before he goes, however, he postures yet again with words. He says that he has reached another midnight and that the dark nature of that witching hour makes him bloodthirsty and makes him desire to decisively take action. But the audience knows better. Hamlet is still not ready to commit to action.

Hamlet's short soliloquy is often used to support the Freudian interpretation of Hamlet's relationship to his mother. Here he speaks of going to her softly, worried that he will not be strong enough to speak his piece. "O heart, lose not thy nature. . . ." Having just assessed his feelings in the language of a traditional revenger in Elizabethan melodrama, Hamlet turns his attention to Gertrude whom he goes to confront as though she were an offending wife to his cuckold.

Glossary

robustious ranting.

groundings the poorer and less critical section of the audience who stood in the pit.

inexplicable dumb shows the unintelligible pantomime preceding the play proper.

Termagant, Herod favorite characters in the old miracle plays, who were always portrayed as blustering tyrants.

candied sugared with hypocrisy.

blood and judgment passion and reason.

pipe a recorder or flute. The stops are the fingerholes.

occulted hidden.

Vulcan's stithy the workshop of the Roman god of fire and metal-working.

heedful note careful observation.

be idle seem crazy.

chameleon's dish The chameleon was supposed to feed on air.

your only jig-maker I am the funniest man alive (ironic).

hautboys oboes.

miching mallecho slinking mischief.

posy of a ring as brief and silly as the inscription inside a ring.

Phoebus' cart Phoebus' chariot. In Greek mythology, Phoebus is Apollo as god of the sun.

Neptune's belonging to Neptune, the Roman god of the sea.

Tellus in Roman mythology, the goddess of the earth.

Hymen in Greek mythology, the god of marriage.

operant powers bodily strength.

wormwood bitterness. (Wormwood is a plant with bitter qualities.)

Tropically the use of a word or words in a figurative sense; figuratively, a trope being a figure of speech.

galled jade a worn-out horse with sores from the rubbing and chafing of a saddle.

withers the highest part of a horse's back, located between the shoulder blades.

chorus in ancient Greek drama, a company of performers whose singing, dancing, and narration provide explanation and elaboration of the main action.

Confederate season suitable opportunity.

Hecate's ban the curse of Hecate, the Greek goddess of the moon, earth, and underground realm of the dead, later regarded as the goddess of sorcery and witchcraft.

forest of feathers plumed hat much worn by players.

turn Turk turn bad.

Provincial roses rosettes for concealing the laces on shoes.

razed slashed for ornamentation.

Damon a perfect friend; in classical legend, Damon and Pythias were friends so devoted to each other that when Pythias, who had been condemned to death, wanted time to arrange his affairs, Damon pledged his life that his friend would return. Pythias returned and both were pardoned.

pajock peacock.

recorders a wind instrument with finger holes and a wedgelike part (a fipple) near the mouthpiece; fipple flute.

purgation the act of purging; Hamlet probably intends a pun—to administer a purgative to get rid of the bile and to purge him of his guilt. The word recalls Hamlet's father, who is in purgatory.

pickers and stealers hands.

recover the wind a hunting phrase—to get to windward.

ventages small holes or openings; vents.

compass the tonal range of a musical instrument.

Nero (A.D. 37-68); notoriously cruel and depraved emperor of Rome (54-68) who killed his own mother.

shent rebuked.

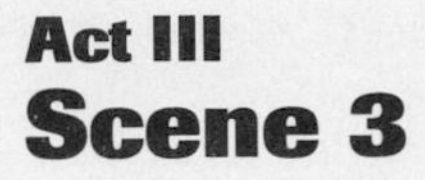

Act III Scene 3

Summary

Fearing that Hamlet is a threat to his life and throne, the King summons Rosencrantz and Guildenstern and instructs them to hurry and take Hamlet to England. The men agree, acknowledging that any threat to Claudius is a threat to the people of Denmark, so they will keep Denmark safe by removing Hamlet from its shores. They leave, and Polonius enters to inform the King that Hamlet is on his way to Gertrude and that Polonius plans to hide there and eavesdrop on the conversation. Promising to report back to Claudius before Claudius retires to bed, Polonius leaves.

Claudius then prays at his private altar, although he says his sin is so great that it renders him incapable of praying. He admits before God that he has committed the "primal eldest curse" by carrying out his "brother's murder." He admits that his contrition is unforgivable since he is unwilling to give up the spoils of his ill-won battles. He begs instead that some divine assistance might bow his knees and soften his heart so that he can ask for forgiveness.

Hamlet enters and sees Claudius in prayer. He recognizes his perfect opportunity to kill Claudius, but stops himself. He remembers that Claudius killed King Hamlet without allowing him any opportunity to make amends for his sins, and that King Hamlet now languishes in purgatory awaiting entry to heaven. Believing that Claudius is praying for forgiveness, Hamlet knows that by killing Claudius now, he would send the King straight to heaven. Claudius would escape the eternal punishment that is his due.

Commentary

From the top of the scene, any ambiguity concerning Claudius' character disappears. He identifies Hamlet as his enemy and plots to have him dispatched to England. He conspires with Polonius to spy on Hamlet yet again. Then, kneeling in prayer before sleeping, the King confesses the depth and severity of his crime. He likens himself to Cain, the primal or first murderer, and admits that he cannot bring himself to ask for God's mercy. "But oh, what form of prayer / can serve my turn?" Claudius knows that he will never abdicate the throne, nor will he give up Gertrude and all "those effects for which I did murder," such as his power and position. He expects to spend eternity in hell.

Hamlet enters as the King kneels with his back toward Hamlet. Hamlet reaches for his sword, and the ambiguity shifts to Hamlet. His Christian morality informs him that because the King appears to pray, he is probably confessing. By ending his life in mid-confession, Hamlet would allow the King to go straight to heaven by virtue of his cleansed soul. Hamlet would prefer to send the King to hell. He has no problem with the immorality of robbing a man of his salvation. Hamlet is capable of imitating King Claudius' cruelty.

Some critics believe that Hamlet vacillates yet again in yet another self-deception of word play. In fact, this moment represents the pivotal point in the play—the moment of truth. Had Hamlet taken charge and acted rather than retreating into his words, he would have prevented the six deaths that follow. Most importantly, the tragic hero might not have met his inevitable end. Then, of course, the play would have been cut short, and no tragedy would exist. Had Hamlet killed Claudius here, he would have more closely resembled Macbeth who murdered innocence—in Macbeth's own words, "Macbeth hath murdered sleep"—by taking the life of an unprotected, unaware King. The action would label Hamlet a villain, not a hero. Claudius survives in order to preserve Hamlet's character.

Glossary

noyance harm.

weal a sound or prosperous state; well-being; welfare.

cease of majesty death of a king.

mortis'd firmly joined.

arras a tapestry wall hanging.

tax him home take him to task.

primal eldest curse that is, the one pronounced upon Cain in for the murder of his brother. Primal here means original.

will desire.

broad blown in full blossom.

hent to grasp; in this case, a time for action.

physic the art or science of healing.

Act III
Scene 4

Summary

As promised, Polonius arrives in Gertrude's room before Hamlet and hides himself behind an arras. He instructs Gertrude to be entirely blunt with her son. Hamlet enters challenging, "Now, Mother, what's the matter?" Gertrude tells him he has badly offended his father, meaning Claudius; Hamlet answers that she has badly offended his father, meaning King Hamlet. Hamlet intimidates Gertrude, and she cries out that he is trying to murder her. Polonius reacts from behind the curtain and yells for help. Hamlet draws his sword and thrusts it through the tapestry, killing Polonius. When Hamlet lifts the wallhanging and discovers Polonius' body, he tells the body that he had believed he was stabbing the King. He then turns his attention to punishing Gertrude. He presses contrasting pictures of Claudius and his brother in Gertrude's face. He points out King Hamlet's godlike countenance and courage, likening Claudius to an infection in King Hamlet's ear. He accuses Gertrude of lustfulness, and she begs him to leave her alone.

King Hamlet's Ghost reappears to Hamlet, but only Hamlet can see him. Hamlet believes that the Ghost has come to chide his tardy son into carrying out the "dread command," but Hamlet then perceives the Ghost as his mother's protector. The Ghost tells his son to be kinder to her. Gertrude is utterly convinced now that her son is hallucinating from a devil-inspired madness, but Hamlet tells her that it is not madness that afflicts him. He begs her to confess her guilt to him and to heaven. At the very least, he begs her, don't sleep with Claudius or let him "go paddling in your neck with his damned fingers."

He asks if she knows that Claudius is sending him to England; she had forgotten. He tells her that he distrusts Rosencrantz and Guildenstern, and that they are undoubtedly taking him to England to do some foul bidding for Claudius. She confesses that she knows about the exile. He bids his mother good night and exits, pulling Polonius' body behind him.

Commentary

Although a closet was a private room in a castle, and a bedroom was meant for receiving visitors, the convention since the late 19th century has been to stage the scene between Hamlet and Gertrude in Gertrude's bedroom. Staging the scene in the closet rather than in a bedroom is more in line with the Freudian psychoanalysis of an Oedipal Hamlet—a man resembling the Greek character Oedipus who bedded his mother and killed his father. If Gertrude received him in her closet, she treated him more as an intimate than as a son.

Up until this scene, one can dismiss the notion that Shakespeare envisioned a prince whose love for his mother was unnatural and itself incestuous. One can rationalize Hamlet's hysteria over Gertrude's marriage to Claudius in light of the Renaissance notion of family honor and the prevailing definitions of incest, which implicated Gertrude and Claudius. But in Act III, Scene 4, no better way exists for the modern thinker to justify Hamlet's behavior than to suppose that he has a Freudian attachment to Gertrude.

Though not the first to cast Hamlet in an Oedipal light, Laurence Olivier popularized the notion of an untoward love between Hamlet and his mother in the 1947 Royal Shakespeare Company production and again in the 1948 film version. In the film, Olivier, playing Hamlet opposite his wife in the role of Gertrude, staged the scene so that it was stripped of all its ambiguities. He dressed Gertrude's bed in satin, and he dressed the Queen, awaiting her son's arrival, in the same suggestively folded satin and silk. The two engage in a verbal exchange that possesses the breathless engagement of foreplay, and Hamlet then presses himself onto his mother in an overtly sexual way. The scene is believable played this way, especially given that Claudius will tell us shortly that Gertrude "lives almost by his looks," and because Hamlet's melodramatic reaction to his father's passing seems so wooden without that underpinning of deep emotion.

Polonius, obscured by the tapestry, has prophetically and ironically placed himself to "silence me e'en here" and quietly observes what transpires between Gertrude and her son. In a passionate outburst, Hamlet threatens his mother, holding up a mirror and saying, "You go not till I set you up a glass / Where you may see the inmost part of you." Gertrude, terrified, assumes that her son intends to murder her and calls for help, to which the hidden Polonius reacts without revealing himself. Still impassioned by his encounter with Gertrude, still inflamed with his sexual tension, Hamlet stabs Polonius. In a grandly impulsive moment, Hamlet has finally acted on his bloodlust, a bloodlust he has sublimated until this moment. According to the post-Freudian interpretation, the need to expiate his misplaced sexual feelings has caused him to stop thinking and act for a change. The irony all belongs to Polonius; he is there to trap Hamlet and finds himself trapped instead. He has said he will silence himself, and he is indeed silenced. There is both simple irony and dramatic irony.

The Ghost's invisibility to Gertrude raises the question of Hamlet's sanity. We can interpret Shakespeare's choice to blind Gertrude to the Ghost's presence and to deafen her ears to her son's insistence that the Ghost exists to mean that Shakespeare fashioned Hamlet as a madman, no longer merely acting the part. Of course, one can also make a case for interpreting the scene as an indictment of Gertrude. She refuses to see the Ghost because of her own guilt. Gertrude's black heart impedes her vision, refusing her the sight of her loving husband. On the other hand, perhaps she does see the Ghost and only pretends not to. Then again, you may interpret the scene as being another proof of Gertrude's innocence.

Up until this scene, judging the extent of Gertrude's complicity in the murder of King Hamlet has been difficult. She now implies that she is entirely innocent. Hamlet counters her horror at Polonius' death with his own accusation

> A bloody deed! Almost as bad, good mother
> As kill a king, and marry his brother.

She answers in innocent surprise, "As kill a king?" Then she asks him, "What have I done, that thou dar'st wag thy tongue / In noise so rude against me?"

If she is guilty, she is also an accomplished actor. According to all appearances, the Ghost was right when he told Hamlet earlier that she was only a follower—a weak woman brainwashed by her need to be loved and cared for. She can discern no other reason for Hamlet to behave in such a way except to hurt her. Gertrude remains incredulous as Hamlet perseveres with his indictment of Claudius as a "murderer and a villain." She does not agree to end Claudius' advances. Hamlet asks her to "prevent the "bloat King" from tempting her to bed again, but she never promises to confess herself and leave the King, and she never tries to convince Hamlet that Claudius is innocent. Nor does she plead for herself or try to make Hamlet see why she chose to marry Claudius.

At the scene's end, as if in a test of his mother's devotion, Hamlet tells Gertrude that Claudius is sending him to England and that he suspects foul play in his uncle's having hired Rosencrantz and Guildenstern to take him there. He says he does not trust them and he confides his fear. Gertrude offers no argument and provides no reassurance. She simply tells him in effect that she'll think about it and lets him leave. In a world where seeming, acting, and playing predominate, judging any character's honesty is difficult. The ambiguities enhance the character, and shroud her in mystery. These characteristics pose a formidable challenge for an actor, making Gertrude a choice role.

Hamlet's immediate acquiescence to his father's will here is significant. Whether the Ghost is real or a figment of his imagination, the old king has successfully yanked Hamlet from the preoccupation with Gertrude that has distracted his quest for retribution. Hamlet leaves Gertrude affectionately. He repeats "Good night" five times and progressively wishes for her peace. He asks her rather than ordering her to keep clear of the king's advances, and he confides his fears about Rosencrantz and Guildenstern. He then takes Polonius' body as a favor to her, not as obligation to the murdered good old man.

Glossary

lay you home to him tell him what's what.

silence me hide myself.

rood a cross as used in crucifixion; specifically, the cross on which Jesus was crucified.

sets a blister In Elizabethan England, prostitutes were sometimes branded with a hot iron.

contraction the marriage contract.

solidity and compound mass the earth.

tristful sorrowful.

index prologue.

counterfeit presentment portrait.

Mercury in Roman mythology, the messenger of the gods; god of commerce, manual skill, eloquence, cleverness, travel, and thievery.

batten to grow fat; thrive; to be well fed or wealthy at another's expense.

apoplex'd paralyzed.

cozen'd cheated.

hoodman-blind blindman's bluff.

so mope be so stupid.

enseam'd greasy, with a pun on semen.

vice of kings caricature of a king. Vice, who represented sin, was a stock character in morality plays.

distemper mental disturbance.

gambol wander; frolic.

unction ointment, salve; used for the act of annointing as in medical treatment or a religious ceremony.

mouse a common term of endearment.

reechy smoky, dirty, foul, or rancid.

paddock toad.

gib tomcat; a male cat, especially a castrated male cat.

enginer engineer.

Act IV
Scene 1

Summary

Claudius, flanked by Rosencrantz and Guildenstern, finds Gertrude and questions her as to Hamlet's whereabouts. She asks to be left alone with the King and, after Rosencrantz and Guildenstern leave, she agitatedly tells him that she has seen a horror. Claudius wants to know what happened and asks after her son's welfare. She answers that Hamlet is madder than a storm at sea, and she describes the killing of Polonius. Realizing that he himself might have been the person hiding behind the tapestry, Claudius deplores Hamlet's violence, but he blames himself for not having been sterner with Hamlet from the beginning. He worries what he will tell his subjects; Gertrude tells him that Hamlet is contrite and has promised to dispose of the body. The King resolves to banish Hamlet quickly and calls to Rosencrantz and Guildenstern. He tells them what has happened and bids them bring Hamlet to him. He tells Gertrude that they must together confide in their wisest friends and find a way to disclose Polonius' death without raising suspicions against themselves.

Commentary

Gertrude explains what has happened in a manner that exemplifies her own ambivalence and ambiguities. Does she really believe Hamlet has lost all reason? Or is she protecting the secret he has just revealed regarding Claudius' guilt—the secret she has promised to keep about King Hamlet's murder? Whether she knew anything about the crime beforehand or if she participated in the plot to take the throne remains unclear. Gertrude's protectiveness toward Hamlet is dubious. She never attempts to shield her son in any meaningful way and describes in inflammatory detail how he killed "the unseen good old man." Even knowing what Hamlet believes about Rosencrantz and Guildenstern does not cause her to entreat the King to find an alternative to sending her son to England with the pair.

Claudius is clearly aware of all the ramifications that attend his reactions to the report. He inquires after Hamlet's health but clearly remains primarily concerned with his own well being. "My soul is full of discord and dismay," he says. He will act quickly on the news, but he is clearly fearful. "His [Hamlet's] liberty is full of threats to all." He hides his fears behind the apparent concern of an uncle, who has been protecting Hamlet out of love but who will protect Hamlet no longer. He will send him to England, and they will tell the people that he is mad. Hamlet's having murdered Polonius will ultimately work to Claudius' advantage. Hamlet must receive punishment, and, although all in Denmark love him as their rightful crown prince in whom rests all hope, the King may now exile the Prince with impunity and without upsetting Gertrude, as even she sees the need to get Hamlet away.

Glossary

brainish apprehension mad notion (that he heard a rat).

out of haunt away from others.

pith marrow.

blank the center spot of a target; bull's-eye.

Act IV
Scene 2

Summary

When Rosencrantz and Guildenstern finally find the Prince and ask him for Polonius, he bewilders them with answers that seem to be riddles. He tells them that sharing information with mere sponges and parasites of the court is beneath him, the son of a king.

Commentary

Hamlet finally reveals his full disdain for Rosencrantz and Guildenstern, saying that he has neither love nor respect for them or their King, to whom he refers as a "thing." Hamlet calls his classmates the worst kind of parasites. The King, Hamlet suggests, keeps Rosencrantz and Guildenstern around "as an ape doth nuts, and in the corner of his jaw; first mout'd to be last swallowed." As long as Claudius needs what the pair can glean of Hamlet's intentions, he will continue to use them; however, Claudius is squeezing them as he would any sponge and will eventually leave them dry again.

Shakespeare uses this as an opportunity to demonstrate Rosencrantz's and Guildenstern's shallow wit. "I understand you not, my lord." Hamlet answers with an outright insult to their collective intelligence by commenting, "a knavish speech sleeps in a foolish ear." Their inferior intelligence fails to discern his ironic, sarcastic language.

Glossary

compounded restored, mingled.

counsel secrets.

first mout'd put into the mouth first in order that all the goodness may be extracted before swallowing.

Act IV
Scene 3

Summary

In a public show of concern, Claudius explains to his assembled courtiers that he cannot jail his nephew because Hamlet remains too popular with the people. A riot would inevitably occur if he punished Hamlet for his part in Polonius' death, so instead he will send the young man into exile.

Rosencrantz enters to report that Hamlet will not reveal Polonius' whereabouts. Guildenstern and the Guards then bring Hamlet in, and Claudius demands to know where Hamlet has put Polonius. Hamlet engages in yet another word play with Claudius, taunting him with images of rotting flesh and the corruption of death. He pointedly tells Claudius that just as a fisherman eats a fish that has eaten a worm that was in the grave eating at a king, every man can progress through the guts of beggar. Then he tells Claudius that even if a messenger was sent to heaven, the messenger could not find the old man. He says that Claudius should seek Polonius in hell, even though the old man would not have arrived there yet either. Instead, Hamlet tells him that, within a month's time, the smell "up the stairs into the lobby" will reveal to them the whereabouts of the body. As attendants go to retrieve Polonius' body, Claudius tells Hamlet that a boat waits to take the Prince to England.

As soon as Hamlet and the guards leave, the King soliloquizes a plea to England to finish the Prince quickly and cleanly. The king of England owes him a favor, and he's calling it in by asking the death of Hamlet.

Commentary

Critics puzzle endlessly over the reason for Hamlet's cat and mouse game with Rosencrantz, Guildenstern, and Claudius over the whereabouts of Polonius' body. Hamlet's apparent madness is both amusing and disturbing. Hamlet is cruel and heartless. He seems to enjoy meting out his measure of torture. His perverse and cruel behavior wholly departs from the heroic figure Hamlet should be. In fact, Hamlet displays characteristics far from heroism in this scene. He exhibits, yet again, a fascination with and terror of death. Unready to face death himself, he imprisons himself more deeply in words and avoids having to kill Claudius. Having murdered Polonius, he has at least been active and need not push himself. Hamlet seems confused, terrified, conflicted; he is coming undone.

The courtiers assemble to learn of Polonius' death, and Claudius maps out the consequences for Hamlet's actions. Hamlet expounds on his worm's meat motif, a repetition of language that Shakespeare uses several times in the play, and that apparently preoccupies Hamlet's mind. The images are gross, troubling, and rife with Hamlet's biting satirical wit. In his rant about the physical realities of death, Hamlet explains that the fact that all men feed the earth and are, therefore, worm's meat is the great equalizer. The King inquires after Polonius' whereabouts, and Hamlet answers that Polonius is at supper—not supping but rather being supped upon: "*Your* worm is your only emperor for diet. We fat all creatures else to fat us, and we fat ourselves for maggots. Your fat king and your lean beggar is but variable service—two dishes but to one table. That's the end."

The moral of his rambling is that, because a man may fish with a worm that has eaten the body of a king, and afterwards eat the fish he has caught, that man has, in essence, devoured a king. Thus, the king passes through the stomach of a beggar and only the worm reigns supreme. Even so, the worm, the king, and the beggar are equal now—they are all dead. Elaborately, Hamlet has called the King a worm.

Hamlet's horror and amusement over death underscore his ambivalence toward his duty. He will reiterate several more times his paradoxical will to die and fear of death before he finally commits his act of vengeance. Yet, he never fails to show his love for the feel of the words he prattles. He allows the words to linger on his tongue; he swills them around and savors them, even when seemingly out of his mind.

Claudius responds by banishing Hamlet to England, and Hamlet tells Claudius that he knows the King's purpose in sending him away. Claudius apparently misses or overlooks the warning and chooses instead to respond to Hamlet's insulting, "Farewell, Mother." Claudius corrects him, offering him an opportunity to apologize. Hamlet then completes the insult by explaining that because man and wife are of one flesh, Claudius is indeed Hamlet's mother. With this insult, Hamlet digs another barb into Claudius about the incest, which always weighs on Hamlet's mind. Claudius finally perceives the depth of the danger Hamlet poses and entreats Rosencrantz and Guildenstern to hurry him to England to get him out of the way. Although unknown to everyone but the audience, Claudius now sees that he must instruct the king of England to kill Hamlet. The lines between good and evil appear clearly now as the gray areas that have masked Claudius' dark purposes vanish. Claudius' evolution into the consummate villain is complete.

Glossary

Deliberate pause a deliberate step, taken after due consideration.

convocation of politic worms a political assembly of worms; an allusion to the Diet of Worms (1521), a convocation held by the Catholic Church to allow Martin Luther to explain his reform of doctrine. He had first set his beliefs forth in Wittenberg, where Hamlet and Horatio have studied.

variable service different courses.

cicatrice scar or wound.

thy free awe your submission even after our armies have been withdrawn.

congruing agreeing.

present immediate; of or at this time.

hectic fever; red or flushed , as with fever.

Act IV
Scene 4

Summary

On his way to England, Hamlet observes Fortinbras leading his troops through Denmark toward Poland. He questions a captain and learns that the Norwegians plan to wage war over a worthless patch of land in Poland. Hamlet lingers behind Rosencrantz and Guildenstern to reflect on the fact that these Norwegians and Poles are willing to die over land worth virtually nothing to anyone. They have left their homes and committed themselves to a principle no more substantive than an eggshell. Yet, he ponders, he possesses sufficient reason to take action against his enemy, but remains paralyzed.

Commentary

Hamlet's soliloquy as he observes the Norwegian soldiers heading for Poland represents *Hamlet's* turning point: "What is a man / If his chief good and market of his time / Be but to sleep and feed? Now, whether it be Bestial oblivion or some craven scruple Of thinking too precisely on th'event—a thought which, quartered, hath but one part wisdom and three parts coward—I do not know Why yet I live to say 'This thing's to do,' Sith I have cause, and will, and strength, and means to do't."

Hamlet finally realizes that his duty to revenge is so great that the end must justify the means. He can no longer escape the necessity for action. Up until now, the consequences of the murder he must commit worried him, and he thought "too precisely on th'event." In weighing the willingness of the Norwegian soldiers to lay down their lives for a worthless piece of land against his own inability to act though motivated by sacred filial duty, he sees that he has stalled long enough. This soliloquy represents Hamlet's last flirtation with words. From here on, he will shed his attachment to the words that cause a deed's "currents to turn awry and lose the name of action."

You can divide the soliloquy into five thematic sections:

The first section identifies Hamlet's mission: revenge. Hamlet says that everything he encounters prompts him to revenge: "How all occasions do inform against me / And spur my dull revenge!"

The second section exhorts him to act. Hamlet must stop overthinking events and recognize in himself the strength, and means to complete the required act

The third section sets Fortinbras' example of how Hamlet should act. "Led by this army of such mass and charge, / Led by a delicate and tender Prince . . . to all that fortune, death and danger dare, / Even for an eggshell." Once again Fortinbras holds up a mirror to his Danish counterpart.

The fourth section specifies Hamlet's perplexity over the Poles' and Norwegians' willingness to die for so little in contrast to his own inability to act on so much.

The fifth section provides resolution. Hamlet resolves to avenge his father at last.

> Oh from this time forth
> My thoughts be bloody or be nothing worth.

Glossary

ranker greater.

in fee outright.

imposthume abscess or festering sore.

fust grow moldy.

fantasy an odd notion; whim.

trick something trifling.

continent containing enough ground.

Act IV
Scene 5

Summary

A court gentleman reports that Ophelia has become pitiably insane. Gertrude refuses to see the girl, but Horatio points out that Ophelia's mental state may attract undue attention to herself and the crown. Gertrude then agrees to speak with Ophelia.

Ophelia enters singing fragments of songs about chaos, death, and unrequited love. The King and Queen both try to speak with her, but she replies only unintelligibly. Claudius comments that her father's death has undoubtedly driven her mad. He asks Horatio to follow and watch her. Then he turns to Gertrude and sums up the troubles that plague Elisinore of late. He recounts his torment over the slaying of Polonius, the secret burial to avoid uprising, the madness of Ophelia, and the arrival of her brother, Laertes, who means to incite rioting over his father's death.

The courtiers hear Laertes and a mob outside attempting to break into the castle. Laertes tells his followers to keep watch at the door, and he angrily asks Claudius to give him his father. Gertrude tries to calm Laertes, but Claudius tells her to let him rail, that they have nothing to fear from the young man. Claudius manages to placate Laertes until Ophelia returns, singing incoherent snippets of a song about a dead old man. Laertes comments that a "young maid's wits" are as fragile and "as mortal as an old man's life." Ophelia distributes flowers to the assembled people, and exits. Laertes, distraught over his sister's condition, finally pays complete attention to what Claudius has to say. The King promises Laertes satisfaction in avenging Polonius' death.

Commentary

Earlier in the play (Act III, Scene 1), Gertrude told Ophelia "And for your part, Ophelia, I do wish / That your good beauties be the happy cause of Hamlet's wildness." Yet now, when Horatio and the gentleman announce Ophelia's request for an audience with Gertrude, Gertrude flatly refuses to see the girl. Gertrude reluctantly agrees to see her only after Horatio and the gentleman explain the piteousness of Ophelia's condition and the danger of Ophelia's behavior to the state.

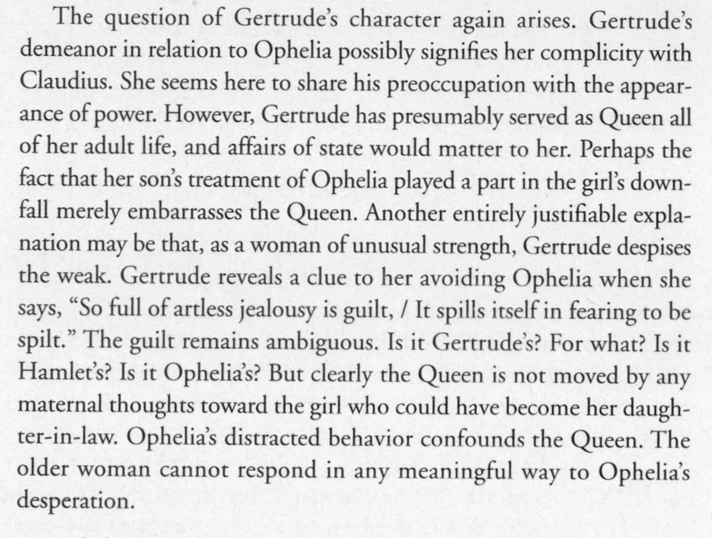

The question of Gertrude's character again arises. Gertrude's demeanor in relation to Ophelia possibly signifies her complicity with Claudius. She seems here to share his preoccupation with the appearance of power. However, Gertrude has presumably served as Queen all of her adult life, and affairs of state would matter to her. Perhaps the fact that her son's treatment of Ophelia played a part in the girl's downfall merely embarrasses the Queen. Another entirely justifiable explanation may be that, as a woman of unusual strength, Gertrude despises the weak. Gertrude reveals a clue to her avoiding Ophelia when she says, "So full of artless jealousy is guilt, / It spills itself in fearing to be spilt." The guilt remains ambiguous. Is it Gertrude's? For what? Is it Hamlet's? Is it Ophelia's? But clearly the Queen is not moved by any maternal thoughts toward the girl who could have become her daughter-in-law. Ophelia's distracted behavior confounds the Queen. The older woman cannot respond in any meaningful way to Ophelia's desperation.

Ophelia's songs all concern unrequited love. The third song, in fact, blatantly indicts a lover who has left his love's bed. "Before you tumbled me, you promised me to wed." This song provides another proof that Ophelia's madness may stem from her having been intimate with Hamlet and then rejected by him. In fact, considering her father's instructions that she not let Hamlet have his way with her, Polonius' death could only exacerbate her guilt. Premarital sex was a sin—a sin compounded by her father's command. If, as some believe, she now carries Hamlet's child, her desperation would be all consuming.

Staging Ophelia's flower distribution with imaginary flowers has become traditional in the modern theater, which generally interpret the flowers as symbolic rather than real. Ophelia gives fennel, symbol of flattery, to King Claudius. She also gives him columbine for ingratitude and infidelity. Rue, for sorrow, she gives to Gertrude; she also offers Gertrude daisy, for springtime and love, and says she lost her own violets, which represent sweetness, when her father died. To Laertes, she gives rosemary, for remembrance, and pansies, for thought, suggesting both their shared history and her lost faculties.

In this scene, Laertes emerges as another foil (opposite) for Hamlet. He, too, has a father to avenge and a woman to protect, but this son wastes no time in thought or word. He threatens the King, only restraining himself when the King promises to assist the younger man in his quest for vengeance. Moral ambivalence does not restrict Laertes, and he willingly risks eternal damnation by acting without hesitation. Laertes, unencumbered by words, ideas, or beliefs, has raised an army against the King to avenge Polonius' death. The King recognizes that Laertes poses a danger to him potentially as great as that posed by Hamlet. He promises Laertes that Hamlet will be eliminated. "Let the great one fall."

Claudius has consistently orchestrated emotions, and has convincingly played the role of concerned King, friend of Polonius, kindly father figure for Ophelia, and dutiful husband to Gertrude. He is lavish with words in this scene, making a great show of his deep empathy for Gertrude, for Laertes, for Ophelia, even for Hamlet. "O Gertrude, Gertrude/When sorrows come, they come not in single spies/But in battalions." Hyperdramatically, he concludes his litany of sufferings they have all had to bear by saying, "O my dear Gertrude, this,/Like to a murdering-piece, in many places/Gives me superfluous death." No one suffers more than Claudius. Contrasted with his soliloquy of Scene 3, where he vows to have Hamlet executed, the speech proves his insincerity to the audience. Now, in blatant dramatic irony, Shakespeare makes the audience privy to the truth before the characters can discover that truth for themselves.

Still, in the political coup of this scene, he wins Laertes' loyalty by urging Gertrude to "let him go" so that he may speak freely. He then gives Laertes free reign, placing himself in apparent jeopardy:

> Make choice of whom your wisest friends you will,
> And they shall hear and judge 'twixt you and me:
> If by direct or by collateral hand
> The find us touch'd, we will our kingdom give,
> Our crown, our life, and all that we call ours
> To you in satisfaction

In his very public show, he manages to manipulate the trust of everyone present.

Glossary

unshaped incoherent.

collection inference.

aim to guess or conjecture.

botch a badly patched place or part

cockle hat a hat adorned with cockle shells and worn by pilgrims.

shoon shoes.

Larded garnished.

Saint Valentine's Day February 14. The old belief was that the first man seen by a maid on that day was destined to be her husband, and vice versa.

dupp'd opened.

Gis corruption for Jesus.

Cock corruption for God

Hugger-mugger secret haste.

buzzers gossipers.

Murdering-piece cannon loaded with grapeshot.

Switzers Swiss mercenary soldiers; in this case, acting as the royal bodyguard.

counter on the false trail (a hunting term); treason.

swoopstake in a clean sweep.

life-rendering pelican The pelican was supposed to feed its young with its own blood.

turn the beam overbalance the scale.

hatchment a diamond-shaped panel bearing the coat of arms of a person who has died.

formal ostentation public ceremony.

Act IV
Scene 6

Summary

Horatio receives letters from a sailor sent by Hamlet. The first letter tells Horatio that pirates beset the ship on which Hamlet was being carried to England. In the ensuing battle, the pirates took Hamlet captive; they treated him well and brought him back to Denmark. He has, in return, promised to do them a favor. The other letters, says Hamlet's first letter, are for Horatio to deliver to the King. After he has made the delivery, Horatio is to come immediately to meet Hamlet; Hamlet tells his friend that he has much news to share.

Commentary

Hamlet's return is a dramatic device providing a *deus ex machina* (a contrived solution to a problem) for the play's plot. Shakespeare uses a problem that seriously threatened Elizabethan/ Jacobean security: the prevalence of pirates. Some critics speculate that Shakespeare means for us to infer that Hamlet, knowing that pirates lurk in every bay, has arranged for the pirates to subvert Rosencrantz and Guildenstern's mission. It is equally likely that the ship bound for England carrying Hamlet and his treacherous "friends" was beset by pirates, and Hamlet, always the smooth talker, was able to connive his own release. In either case, the outcome is critical to the play's action. Only by returning to the center of the conflict can Hamlet create the forces that drive the climax, denouement, and resolution.

Glossary

an't if it.

compelled valour bravery that stems from necessity.

thieves of mercy merciful thieves.

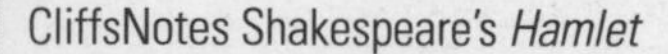

Act IV
Scene 7

Summary

Claudius confirms that Hamlet killed Polonius, though seeking to take Claudius' life. Laertes can't understand why Claudius didn't punish Hamlet for such capitol crimes. Claudius explains that he has restrained himself, even though he has no intention of letting Hamlet get away with his crimes.

At this point, a messenger arrives with the letters Hamlet has sent in Horatio's care. Now knowing that Hamlet is still alive, Claudius offers Laertes an opportunity to show his love for Polonius by joining him in a plot to kill Hamlet by engaging in swordplay with him. Claudius promises to arrange a fencing match between Laertes and Hamlet. Hamlet will use a fencing foil, but Laertes' foil will have an unblunted point. Thus, Laertes can kill Hamlet in front of an audience, and it will appear to be an accident; no one will know it is murder. Laertes shares his own plan to dip his sword in a poison so lethal that a minor scratch will cause instant death. Claudius adds yet another safeguard: He will poison a goblet of wine for Hamlet to drink, so that even if Laertes fails to draw blood, Hamlet will die.

Gertrude interrupts their plotting with her report of Ophelia's drowning. She describes the young woman's death graphically, explaining how she had fallen in the brook while weaving flower garlands; the willow tree branch on which she was sitting broke so that she tumbled into the water. Ophelia's clothing carried her afloat for a time, but eventually she sank to her death. Laertes finds his grief uncontrollable, and he runs out in a rage. Claudius and Gertrude follow him, ostensibly to quell his anger.

Commentary

Claudius struts for Laertes in this scene, but, if we believe what he says, he also demonstrates his ability to care. Caring would mitigate his evil and add to the paradox inherent in his character. As shown in his prayer scene in Act III, Claudius has a Christian conscience even if he is incapable of satisfying it. In this scene he demonstrates that he may also be a devoted husband who prizes the emotional well being of his beloved wife. Despite his knowledge that Hamlet is a great danger to him, he tells Laertes that he has chosen not to hurt his "son" because the Queen "lives almost by his looks," and Claudius lives almost for the Queen.

However, Claudius' entirely self-serving evil becomes immediately apparent when he explains to Laertes his second reason for not punishing Hamlet for Polonius' murder: the great love the country has for Hamlet, which would not look kindly on the King who threatened him. Scholars contend that succession to the throne of Denmark was determined by a vote. Knights of the realm chose from candidates who petitioned for the throne. According to the Scandinavian legend, Gertrude's father was the king before King Hamlet. King Hamlet was selected by his predecessor to marry the princess, and the marriage clinched his election to the monarchy. If these conditions exist, Claudius clearly cannot afford to lose face before his knights, and he cannot afford to lose Gertrude; nor can he jeopardize his tenuous popularity by risking a backlash against the throne.

By exercising his skill with posturing emotions, Claudius convinces Laertes that he has restrained his actions toward Hamlet for reasons that make him look like a kind man and a responsible monarch. The speech wins Laertes over, and Claudius gains a powerful ally. Now that his plan to have Hamlet executed by the English king has failed, Claudius needs Laertes' assistance in eliminating Hamlet.

The two hatch a grand scheme to ensure that Hamlet will not escape again. As in the murder of King Hamlet, undetectable poison serves as the weapon of choice for Claudius. Like his malicious intentions, which he masks with sweet sentiments, Claudius' penchant for poison proves his insidiousness. Hamlet's statement in his letter that he has returned "naked" to Denmark leads to the conclusion that he will face Claudius alone. The conspirators have every reason to expect success in their plot, especially as Laertes is as renowned for his swordsmanship as is Hamlet.

Once again Laertes serves as the perfect foil for Prince Hamlet. He minces no words and loses no time on regret. His deep anguish over the loss of his father and sister commits itself to murder. Laertes is immediately ready, able, and willing to act. A sympathetic and formidable adversary for the sympathetic and formidable prince, Laertes will garner as much support from the audience as Hamlet will, and the confrontation will be doubly moving as the audience will be torn in its allegiance.

A note on Ophelia's characterization: Although Gertrude reports that Ophelia fell in the stream and drowned, there is evidence that her death is a suicide. The first proof can be found in her present state. Faced with the reality of premarital sex and a manless future—Hamlet did not want her, her father was dead, and her judgmental brother was in France—Ophelia would have recognized no other solution but suicide. Another proof is evident in the circumstances of her death. Some critics believe her drowning proves that she was pregnant and, consequently, committed suicide. While no concrete evidence of a pregnancy exists, critics point to the fact that in the 16th and 17th centuries, the conventional suicide method for an unmarried pregnant woman was drowning.

Claudius' evil ambition has infected Laertes, despite the fact that Laertes has been in Paris, away from Claudius' influence. Hamlet has returned to put right what he perceives as Claudius' wrongs, but by causing the deaths of Polonius and Ophelia, Hamlet has become an instrument of the evil he opposes. That something is "rotten in the State of Denmark," as Marcellus observed in Act II, is now clear throughout the kingdom.

Glossary

unsinew'd weak.

conjunctive closely united.

timber'd made of wood that is too light.

checking at swerving aside from; a term in hawking.

livery the characteristic clothing worn by members of a particular group or trade.

his sables and his weeds dignified robes.

incorps'd and demi-natur'd an integral part of the body.

scrimers fencers.

passages of proof proven by events.

snuff accumulation of smoldering wick that caused the candle to smoke and burn less brightly.

plurisy excess.

quick o' the ulcer the heart of the matter.

sanctuarize give sanctuary to a murderer.

foils long, thin swords with a button on the point to prevent injury, used in fencing.

unbated not blunted.

pass of practice a treacherous thrust or a warming-up exercise.

mountebank quack doctor.

cataplasm a poultice, often medicated.

simples medicinal herbs.

Under the moon To be most effective, herbs are gathered by moonlight.

gall scratch, draw blood.

nonce occasion.

hoar gray.

coronet weeds garlands of flowers.

envious silver malicious branch.

lauds hymns of praise.

indu'd endowed, belonging to.

lay song.

douts extinguishes; literally, do out.

ACT V
Scene 1

Summary

Two gravediggers (called clowns) discuss the burial for which they are digging. An inquest has declared the corpse fit for Christian burial. The First Gravedigger argues that the dead woman deserves no such indulgence, because she drowned herself and is not worthy of salvation. The other gravedigger explains, using misplaced words (malapropisms) and incorrect syntax, that she deserves defending. He reasons that her gentlewoman's rank should earn her a Christian burial. Their dialogue, played for humor, invokes references to the Bible and to the art of gallows-making, where builders build a frame that outlives its tenants. While the Second Gravedigger goes to fetch some liquor, Hamlet and Horatio enter and question the First Gravedigger.

The gravedigger and Hamlet engage in a witty game of "chop-logic"—repartée composed of a series of questions and answers. The gravedigger tells Hamlet that he has been digging graves since the day Old King Hamlet defeated Old King Fortinbras, the very birthday of Prince Hamlet—"he that's mad, and sent to England"—thirty years ago.

Hamlet drives the comic dialectic (a dialectic is a method of examining an idea in which every question posed poses a new question). He mulls again over the nature of life and death, and the great chasm between the two states. He tosses skulls and parries with the possibilities of what each may have been in life. He asks the gravedigger whose grave he is in, and the gravedigger plays with puns, finally asserting that the grave is one who was a woman. Hamlet has no idea to whom the grave belongs.

When Hamlet finds a particular skull, he asks the gravedigger whose it might be. The gravedigger tells him the skull belonged to Yorick, the king's jester. "I knew him, Horatio, a fellow of infinite jest, of most excellent fancy." He dwells on the subject of death and the fact that all men are worm's meat, that all that lives will one day die, and that no rank or money can change the equality of death. Death transforms even great kings like Alexander into trivial objects.

Hamlet and Horatio then observe that the Queen, King, and Laertes arrive among a group of mourners escorting a coffin. He asks whose coffin they're following, and hides with Horatio to listen in to what's happening. He notes that the funeral is not a full Christian rite but that the body is being interred in sacred ground.

Laertes argues with the priest over Ophelia's burial. Claudius' command at inquest, he argues, should grant her all the rites of a Christian burial. The priest refuses, saying that, because she committed suicide, he must deny Ophelia the requiem mass and other trappings of a Christian burial, even though Ophelia will be buried on sacred ground. Laertes insults the priest.

When Ophelia's body is placed into the grave, Hamlet watches the Queen strew the coffin with flowers. "Sweets to the sweet," she says; "I hoped thou shouldst have been my Hamlet's wife." Hamlet now realizes that it is Ophelia who lies dead in the casket, and he attacks Laertes, who has just cursed Hamlet and thrown himself into the grave. Hamlet and Laertes argue over who loved Ophelia best. Laertes tries to strangle Hamlet, but attendants separate them.

Gertrude decries her son's madness. Claudius asks Horatio to look after Hamlet and promises Laertes immediate satisfaction. He instructs Gertrude to have her son watched, implying that another death will serve as Ophelia's memorial.

Commentary

The most serious act in the play begins with the broadest comedy in Shakespeare's repertory. The tragic conclusion begins with two gravediggers—usually played as country bumpkins—who banter over the circumstances of Ophelia's death. The characters are derived from a tradition of performance called *Commedia del'Arte,* an originally Italian clowning technique that was very popular in Renaissance theater throughout Europe. This dialogue introduces the audience to the notion that Ophelia has killed herself, even though Gertrude's report made the death seem accidental. The gravediggers indulge in a spate of black comedy that culminates in Hamlet's matching wits with the adeptly paradoxical First Gravedigger.

Shakespeare's juxtaposing of lofty concepts such as theological law against the lowliness of the gravediggers' station works as the essence of this scene's comedy. The First Gravedigger employs clever malapropisms and provides yet another foil for Hamlet—a base commoner whose sense of irony and paradox matches Hamlet's own, but amuses rather than tortures the thinker.

Shakespeare reiterates his theme of death as the great equalizer in this scene. He also explores the absolute finality of death. Each of the gravediggers' references to death foreshadows Hamlet's imminent participation in several deaths, including his own. Hamlet and the gravedigger humorously discuss Hamlet's preoccupation with worm's meat and the destruction of time. The gravedigger mentions Cain and "the first foul murder," which reminds the audience that Claudius, too, is a brother killer.

The question of Ophelia's suicide alludes to a contemporary court case wherein the court barred Sir James Hall from receiving a Christian burial because he killed himself. Shakespeare undoubtedly built this part of the scene deliberately to show his support for the court's decision. The explanation of Ophelia's burial offered in most criticisms is that the grave is on the periphery of the sacred ground, in an area reserved for those whose Christianity might be questionable. Yorick for one. This is supported by the fact that there are so many skulls in the grave; it's a common grave, not an individualized, consecrated resting place.

Laertes and Hamlet's fight symbolizes Hamlet's internal struggle to control his inability to act. Hamlet's challenging Laertes, whom he calls "a very noble youth," is uncharacteristically rash. Faced with his mirror opposite, a man who is all impassioned action and few words, Hamlet grapples to prove that he loved Ophelia though he was unable to demonstrate his feelings for her.

Glossary

Clowns rustics. The word indicates that these roles were played by comic actors.

crowner coroner.

se offendendo in self-defense.

argal therefore.

will he, nill he willy-nilly, whether he wishes or not.

arms a coat of arms, being a group of emblems and figures arranged on and around a shield and serving as the special insignia of a person, family, or institution.

stoup a drinking cup; tankard.

Intil into.

jowls bumps.

Cain's jaw-bone the jawbone of an ass, with which Cain is supposed to have killed Abel.

politician plotter, schemer.

chapless jawless.

mazzard slang for head (literally, drinking bowl).

loggats skittles or ninepins, a British game in which a ball is bowled at nine wooden pins.

quiddities trifling distinctions; quibbles.

quilets quibbles.

tenures titles to property.

sconce a slang word for head (literally, blockhouse).

pair of indentures agreements in duplicate.

conveyance the document by which real property is transferred from one person to another; deed.

assurance a pun on conveyance of property by deed and security.

quick living.

galls his kibe scrapes his heel.

whoreson a scoundrel; knave; a general epithet of abuse (literally, bastard).

gorge stomach (literally, throat or gullet).

gibes jests.

chapfallen a pun; disheartened, depressed, or humiliated (literally, having one's lower jaw hanging down).

bung-hole a hole in a barrel or keg through which liquid can be poured in or drawn out.

flaw a sudden, brief gust of wind, often with rain or snow; a squall.

fordo destroy.

couch lie concealed; to hide.

crants wreaths.

maiden strewments flowers strewn on a girl's grave.

Pelion, Olympus, and Ossa mountains in Greece; in Greek mythology, the Titans (giant deities) piled Pelion on Ossa and both on Olympus in a futile attempt to reach and attack the gods in heaven.

splenetive full of spleen, hot-tempered.

Woo't colloquial and familiar form of wilt thou.

eisel vinegar.

the burning zone the sun.

Act V
Scene 2

Summary

A calmer Hamlet recounts the events leading up to his escape from the plot to kill him. He says that he is convinced now more than ever that divine providence governs man's life, and that things happen as they are meant to happen. He tells Horatio that the night before the pirates took him, he found himself unable to sleep. He used this opportunity to investigate Rosencrantz and Guildenstern's cabin. Groping about in the darkness, he discovered letters addressed to the English King, which he managed to open with surreptitious skill. To his surprise, he read that Claudius had requested the king of England to imprison and behead Hamlet as quickly as possible. Horatio remains incredulous until Hamlet hands him the letter. While Horatio reads, Hamlet continues. He says that he immediately conjured a brilliant plan. He composed a second set of letters in the flowery style of the original ordering that Rosencrantz and Guildenstern be killed. He sealed the letters with his father's State Seal, which he carried in his purse. Rosencrantz and Guildenstern do not know that Hamlet has replaced the letters, and thus, according to Hamlet, their demise will be due to their own actions in delivering the letters to the English king.

Claudius' behavior horrifies Horatio. "Why what a king is this!" he exclaims. Hamlet reminds him that this same king killed the rightful king, made Gertrude a whore, and robbed Hamlet of his own birthright, all in one fell stroke. Horatio worries that Claudius will learn the outcome of events in England too quickly, but Hamlet assures him that he will now act expeditiously to eliminate the King.

Hamlet says he is only sorry about one thing now: That he has had to engage Laertes in the business. Osric, a courtier, enters and Hamlet mocks the man's flamboyance. Osric tells Hamlet that Laertes invites the Prince to duel with him. The King has wagered that Hamlet will win, and Osric is to return and report whether Hamlet will accept. He does. After Osric's exit, a lord enters with instructions from the King to see if Hamlet wants more time before meeting Laertes. Hamlet says he is ready whenever the King wants to get started. Then the lord tells Hamlet that the Queen wishes him to extend Laertes a pre-duel overture of friendship. Hamlet agrees, and the lord exits.

Horatio feels uneasy about the duel and suggests that Hamlet could lose. Hamlet shrugs off any possibility of Laertes' winning, but says that, in any event, one cannot avoid one's destiny. Hamlet must do what he must do. All that matters is being prepared for the inevitable. "The readiness is all."

With great flourish, the scene is set for the duel. The King calls Hamlet and Laertes together and has them begin the duel by clasping hands. Hamlet asks Laertes to forgive his earlier acts of madness at Ophelia's grave. He further claims that his madness, not he himself, is responsible for Polonius' death, and he begs pardon for the crime. Laertes remains stiff and suspicious in his response, but says he bears Hamlet no grudge.

Osric brings the swords, and Laertes makes a show of choosing his; Hamlet asks only if the one he has chosen is the same length as the others. The King sets wine out for the duelists to drink and holds up the cup intended for Hamlet. Laertes and Hamlet fence for a moment until Hamlet asks for a judgment call from Osric the referee. Osric proclaims a hit in Hamlet's favor, and Claudius holds up Hamlet's goblet and takes a drink. With high pomp, Claudius drops a pearl, his gift to Hamlet, into the wine.

When Hamlet hits Laertes a second time, Laertes protests that it is a mere touch. Claudius assures Gertrude that, "Our son shall win." Gertrude agrees. She takes Hamlet's wine, wipes his brow, and offers him a drink, which he refuses. She then toasts her son. Claudius asks her not to drink, but she does and then wipes Hamlet's brow one more time.

Laertes tells Claudius that the time has come to hit Hamlet with the poisoned tip. Claudius disagrees. In an aside, Laertes expresses a reluctance to hit Hamlet, but Hamlet accuses him of dallying and presses for a third bout. The two fight again and Laertes wounds Hamlet with the poisoned tip. Both drop their swords and, in the scuffle, Hamlet grabs Laertes' sword and Laertes picks up Hamlet's. Hamlet hits Laertes with the poisoned sword. Gertrude swoons. Hamlet sees the Queen fall and anxiously asks, "How does the Queen?" The King assures him that she is faint because of the blood, but Gertrude cries out that the drink has poisoned her. Outraged, Hamlet orders the doors locked so that the King cannot escape. Laertes reveals the murder plot to Hamlet and explains that the poisoned sword now rests in Hamlet's hands.

In a fury, Hamlet runs the sword through Claudius, yelling, "Venom do thy work." Before Claudius dies, Hamlet pours the poisoned wine down the King's throat. Hamlet then goes to Laertes, who is nearly dead. The two forgive one another so that neither will prevent the other from entering heaven. Laertes dies, and Horatio rushes to Hamlet's side.

Hamlet tells Horatio that he is dead, and asks that Horatio "tell my story." Osric announces the sound of an approaching army, which means that Fortinbras has arrived in Denmark after attacking the Poles. Hamlet tells Horatio to ensure that the Danish crown passes to Fortinbras.

With the words "The rest is silence," Hamlet dies. Horatio wishes him a gentle rest and turns his attention to Fortinbras and the English ambassadors, who have also arrived to announce that the English government has executed Rosencrantz and Guildenstern. Fortinbras, appalled by the sight of the mayhem that greets him, "with sorrow" recognizes his right to wear the crown of Denmark, which Horatio will corroborate with Hamlet's words.

Fortinbras orders that Hamlet be given military honors, "with music and rite of war." He orders his soldiers to carry the bodies out, and the play ends.

Commentary

Maynard Mack says that in the last act of the play "Hamlet accepts his world and we discover a different man." He has existed outside of the corrupt system, and yet, he has been unable to resist being drawn in. The Ghost sealed Hamlet's fate when he challenged him to "remember me." In this final scene, the maelstrom finally catches Hamlet stripped of his words, and at the mercy of his "bare bodkin." He maneuvered around the world of "seems" and "acts" and "plays" as long as he could, and tried to beat this world by using its own tactics. He feigned madness and betrayed the woman he ostensibly loves, her father, and his school chums. He committed three cold-blooded murders and sent Ophelia to her death. He had thought he towered above such dirty fighting, but found himself swept into it. He must now face the inevitable. As Mack says, Hamlet has finally "learned, and accepted, the boundaries in which human action, human judgment, are enclosed."

We recognize Hamlet's change in the first part of the scene when he explains to Horatio with complete dismissal how he sent Rosencrantz and Guildenstern to their deaths. The calculating premeditation of his actions is a complete reversal of the Hamlet we have come to know. Horatio's next comment indicates that he is horrified. He says, "So Guildenstern and Rosencrantz go to't," meaning that they go to their deaths, to which Hamlet counters

> Why man, they did make love to this employment.
> They are not near my conscience. Their defeat
> Does by their own insinuation grow.

Hamlet has transformed himself from a man who wallows in self-recrimination into one who can blithely justify cold-blooded betrayal and murder. More significantly, Hamlet has become a man who assumes he can take responsibility for righting all the wrongs created by his corrupt uncle's usurpation of the old order by killing Claudius and reclaiming the throne.

Shakespeare juxtaposes Osric's entrance against Hamlet's resolve to act. As the representative of Claudius' court, Osric embodies all that is rotten in the state of Denmark. According to Hamlet, Osric is one of the many superficial fashionable people overrunning Denmark in these frivolous times. This ostentation is the canker of Denmark's nature, and Hamlet is sure that he is ready to obliterate it. Osric, about whom Hamlet says, " 'tis a vice to know him," represents the evil Hamlet spoke of in Act II when he observed the court in drunken revel. Speaking about the party going on is the kind that causes the rest of the world to see Denmark as a country of drunken louts. Hamlet presumes it his duty to obliterate the King's evil, and that includes Osric.

After Osric and the lord have both been assured that Hamlet will participate in the duel at the King's pleasure, Horatio urges caution. Nevertheless, Hamlet—in a speech that resonates with the resolve he found in Act IV Scene 4 when he watched the Norwegians head toward Poland—states unequivocally how prepared he is to take on all his responsibilities.

His words paraphrase the Biblical passage that no sparrow falls without God's knowledge: "There is special providence in the fall of a sparrow. If it be now, 'tis not to come; if it be not to come, it will be now; if it be not now, yet it will come—the readiness is all. Since no man of aught he leaves knows, what is't to leave betimes? Let it be." Here, Hamlet portrays the consummate existentialist, facing his struggle to play out with dignity and honor the part that has been written for him on the stars. He truly exists in the moment, and will seize it.

Having declared his intentions, Hamlet enters the ring amid great fanfare, and begins his journey by making the first move toward reconciliation with Laertes. He realizes that he must do so at this juncture. Hamlet recognizes himself in Laertes, and needs to release himself from the burden of self-loathing by forgiving and being forgiven by Laertes. He said earlier of Laertes

> But I am sorry, good Horatio,
> That to Laertes I forgot myself,
> For by the image of my cause, I see
> The portraiture of his. I'll court his favours.
> But sure the bravery of his grief did put me
> Into towering passion.

By reaching out to Laertes, Hamlet reconciles the conflicting aspects of his own nature, freeing himself for what he must do. Some other hurdles still lie ahead of him, but he believes he is ready, which is half the battle for him—if not quite the entire battle.

Laertes' resolve to kill Hamlet as punishment for the deaths of Polonius and Ophelia mirrors Hamlet's perceived newfound freedom from words.

> I am satisfied in nature
> Whose motive in this case should stir me most
> To my revenge; but in my terms of honour
> I stand aloof, and will no reconcilement
> Till by some elder masters of known honour
> I have a voice and precedent of peace
> To keep my name ungored.

In the end, the readiness is indeed what matters most. And so, the fight begins.

From the start of the fight, Hamlet is clearly aware that the duel is to the death and not just "play." He recognizes the direness of the situation and understands that Laertes presents his final challenge. What remains unclear is whether Hamlet knows about Claudius' and Laertes' plot. Does he, for example, refuse the wine that Claudius offers him because he suspects danger? All he says is "I'll play this bout first, set it by awhile." After Gertrude takes her fatal sip, he says, "I dare not drink yet, Madam, by and by." Is Hamlet afraid that the wine will dull his fencing skill? Or does he guess that the wine poses a danger? He does not remark at all when the King says, "Gertrude, do not drink!" Does he not hear the King, or does he choose to ignore the warning? Laertes presents a sympathetic and formidable adversary for the sympathetic and formidable Prince. Laertes will garner as much support from the audience as Hamlet will, and the confrontation will be doubly moving as the audience will be torn in its allegiance

In production, Claudius' directive becomes a pivotal moment. How the director and actor interpret the four words determine the tenor of the rest of the play. If Claudius mutters the line under his breath, then he has no thought to protect Gertrude or to warn Hamlet. If he cries it out, the director must find a reasonable way for Hamlet to react, one that reflects a commitment to Hamlet's being aware of the poison—does he want Gertrude to die?—or a commitment to his being tunnel-visioned, intent on his mission to "end the heartache and the thousand natural shocks that flesh is heir to." Is Gertrude's death "a consummation devoutly to be wished," or is it a shocking blow that crushes any will Hamlet may have had left to live?

Still another question that must be asked and answered in production: Is Gertrude's death an accident or suicide? Here the answer to the question about how much Gertrude knows concerning King Hamlet's murder is crucial. Does she know that Claudius has poisoned Hamlet's cup, and does she drink from it to save Hamlet? If she was innocent before Hamlet came to her closet and killed Polonius, did she believe Hamlet's raving, mad indictment of her husband? Either way, she dies, and her death spurs Hamlet into finally doing what he has said he will do since the beginning of the play—kill Claudius

Laertes' death and revelation serve as another catalyst to Hamlet's resolve. When Laertes' is cut by his own sword, again he speaks for Hamlet, "Why, as a woodcock to mine own springe, Osric. I am justly killed with mine own treachery." Traps from which they cannot extricate themselves catch both Hamlet and Laertes. They must commit murder in order to uphold the blood feud they have sworn, but they are both Christians and bound by Christian morality to abhor violence. Each must fall due to his own treachery, and each must die and leave the greater good to mitigate any consequences he will face in his afterlife.

For all his great rhetoric, Hamlet has still not taken charge of the deed he must perform: Claudius still lives. Now, wading through the bodies of the people whose deaths he has caused by his hesitancy, Hamlet faces the final truth he cannot avoid. Laertes bears the news:

> It is here Hamlet. Hamlet, thou art slain,
> No medicine in the world can do thee good,
> In thee there is not half an hour of life —
> The treacherous instrument is in they hand,
> Unbated and envenomed. The foul practice
> Hath turned itself on me; lo, here I lie,
> Never to rise again. Thy mother's poisoned —
> I can no more—the king, the king's to blame.

Knowing that he is a dead man, and realizing, at last, exactly what fate the stars hold for him, Hamlet attacks Claudius with the vengeance that has resided in his heart all along. He stabs Claudius and, for extra measure, pours the poison down the King's throat. To heighten the drama as Claudius' death approaches, a chorus of the assembled court cries, "Treason, treason!" and Claudius begs, "Oh yet defend me friends, I am but hurt." A tense moment occurs as Hamlet must consider that his adoring public may perceive him a villain. After all, executing a king who rules by Divine Right constitutes high treason. Yet the court does not stir, and Claudius dies. Hamlet's sense of righteous vengeance fortifies him.

Now Hamlet must face his own death. In order to shuffle off his mortal coil, Hamlet must make peace. He first reconciles with his foil Laertes. The two men exchange pardons, and they consign one another to Christian heaven by releasing themselves from culpability for the lives they have taken. The one task Hamlet must still complete is to find a conduit for the words that have kept him alive, which have been as much his sustenance as his torture. So he asks the loyal Horatio to tell his story.

Horatio, Hamlet's calmer mirror image, now carries the responsibility of juggling the conflict between thinking and doing, between words and action. Hamlet gives his "dying voice" to Fortinbras, who has arrived in Denmark from fighting in Poland just as Hamlet prepares to take his final breath. In Fortinbras, Hamlet recognizes a kindred spirit who can appreciate the significance of the words and who can restore honor to Denmark as he claims the throne. Hamlet then releases himself to death once and for all. "The rest is silence."

Fortinbras takes immediate charge, listening to the story Horatio tells and immediately ordering his soldiers to clean up the mess. He replaces the confusion with calm by ordering a hero's funeral for Hamlet. He will obliterate the corruption of Claudius' reign, and end what Horatio reported as the "carnal, bloody and unnatural acts" that have ruled Denmark.

We know that all will be well because the last words in the play belong to strong, unequivocal Fortinbras:

> Take up the bodies. Such a sight as this
> Becomes the field, but here shows much amiss.

Theme

The final scene also completes the revenge triangle. All the sons of the murdered fathers (King Hamlet, King Fortinbras, and Polonius) have seen vengeance served. The sons have appeased the medieval code of honor while satisfying the Christian expectation of forgiveness. Most importantly, Hamlet is finally a warrior. Like Achilles' son Phyrrus, to whom the First Player referred in Act II, Hamlet has stopped standing "like a neutral to his will and matter." After his stunned pause, Phyrrus took a "rousèd revenge" and killed King Priam. So Hamlet has overcome his paralysis and has killed King Claudius. And, like Phyrrus, he will be buried with the hero's glory that he has finally earned.

Glossary

mutines mutineers.

bilboes long iron bars with sliding shackles, for fettering prisoners' feet.

sea-gown a skirted garment with short sleeves, worn by seamen.

bugs terrors, nightmares.

wheaten garland a garland made of stalks of wheat; a symbol of prosperity.

ordinant provident.

changeling a child secretly put in the place of another; especially, in folk tales, one exchanged in this way by fairies.

angle fishing line.

cozenage treachery.

waterfly an insect without apparent purpose.

chough a chatterer.

imputation reputation.

meed a merited recompense or reward.

unfellowed without equal.

imponed staked; wagered.

poniards daggers.

assigns appurtenances.

hangers straps by which the rapier was hung from the girdle.

twelve for nine In a match of twelve bouts (instead of the usual nine), Laertes will win by at least three up.

breathing time time of exercise.

dug a female animal's nipple or teat; vulgarly, a woman's breast

drossy frivolous; worthless stuff; rubbish.

tune of the time fashionable jargon.

yesty collection frothy collection of catchwords.

gain-giving misgiving.

Stick fiery off stand out brightly.

quit in answer score a return hit.

union a large pearl.

fat out of condition, sweaty.

mutes or audience silent spectators.

antique Roman The ancient Roman was ever ready to commit suicide when confronted with calamity.

quarry heap of slain.

CHARACTER ANALYSES

The following character analyses delve into the physical, emotional, and psychological traits of the literary work's major characters so that you might better understand what motivates these characters. The writer of this study guide provides this scholarship as an educational tool by which you may compare your own interpretations of the characters. Before reading the character analyses that follow, consider first writing your own short essays on the characters as an exercise by which you can test your understanding of the original literary work. Then, compare your essays to those that follow, noting discrepancies between the two. If your essays appear lacking, that might indicate that you need to re-read the original literary work or re-familiarize yourself with the major characters.

Hamlet

Hamlet is an enigma. No matter how many ways critics examine him, no absolute truth emerges. Hamlet breathes with the multiple dimensions of a living human being, and everyone understands him in a personal way. Hamlet's challenge to Guildenstern rings true for everyone who seeks to know him: "You would pluck out the heart of my mystery." None of us ever really does.

The conundrum that is Hamlet stems from the fact that every time we look at him, he is different. In understanding literary characters, just as in understanding real people, our perceptions depend on what we bring to the investigation. Hamlet is so complete a character that, like an old friend or relative, our relationship to him changes each time we visit him, and he never ceases to surprise us. Therein lies the secret to the enduring love affair audiences have with him. They never tire of the intrigue.

The paradox of Hamlet's nature draws people to the character. He is at once the consummate iconoclast, in self-imposed exile from Elsinore Society, while, at the same time, he is the adulated champion of Denmark—the people's hero. He has no friends left, but Horatio loves him unconditionally. He is angry, dejected, depressed, and brooding; he is manic, elated, enthusiastic, and energetic. He is dark and suicidal, a man who loathes himself and his fate. Yet, at the same time, he is an existential thinker who accepts that he must deal with life on its own terms, that he must choose to meet it head on. "We defy augury. There is special providence in the fall of a sparrow."

Hamlet not only participates in his life, but astutely observes it as well. He recognizes the decay of the Danish society (represented by his Uncle Claudius), but also understands that he can blame no social ills on just one person. He remains aware of the ironies that constitute human endeavor, and he savors them. Though he says, "Man delights not me," the contradictions that characterize us all intrigue him. "What a piece of work is a man! How noble in reason, how infinite in faculties, in form and moving how express and admirable, in action how like an angel, in apprehension how like a god!"

As astutely as he observes the world around him, Hamlet also keenly critiques himself. In his soliloquys he upbraids himself for his failure to act as well as for his propensity for words.

Hamlet is infuriatingly adept at twisting and manipulating words. He confuses his so-called friends Rosencrantz and Guildenstern—whom he trusts as he "would adders fang'd"—with his dissertations on ambition, turning their observations around so that they seem to admire beggars more than their King. And he leads them on a merry chase in search of Polonius' body. He openly mocks the dottering Polonius with his word plays, which elude the old man's understanding. He continually spars with Claudius, who recognizes the danger of Hamlet's wit but is never smart enough to defend himself against it.

Words are Hamlet's constant companions, his weapons, and his defenses. In *Rosencrantz and Guildenstern are Dead,* a play that was later adapted into a film, playwright and screenplaywright Tom Stoppard imagines the various wordplays in *Hamlet* as games. In one scene, his characters play a set of tennis where words serve as balls and rackets. Hamlet is certainly the Pete Sampras of wordplay.

And yet, words also serve as Hamlet's prison. He analyzes and examines every nuance of his situation until he has exhausted every angle. They cause him to be indecisive. He dallies in his own wit, intoxicated by the mix of words he can concoct; he frustrates his own burning desire to be more like his father, the Hyperion. When he says that Claudius is " . . .no more like my father than I to Hercules" he recognizes his enslavement to words, his inability to thrust home his sword of truth. No mythic character is Hamlet. He is stuck, unable to avenge his father's death because words control him.

> What an ass am I! This is most brave,
> That I, the son of a dear murderèd
> Prompted to my revenge by heaven and hell,
> Must like a whore unpack my heart with words,
> And fall-a-cursing like a very drab,
> A scallion!

Hamlet's paradoxical relationship with words has held audiences in his thrall since he debuted in 1603 or so. But the controversy of his sexual identity equally charms and repels people.

Is Hamlet in love with his mother? The psychoanalytic profile of the character supports Freud's theory that Hamlet has an unnatural love for his mother. Hamlet unequivocally hates his stepfather and abhors the incestuous relationship between Claudius and Gertrude. But whether jealousy prompts his hatred, whether his fixation on his mother causes his inability to love Ophelia, and whether he lusts after Gertrude all depend on interpretation. And no interpretation is flawless.

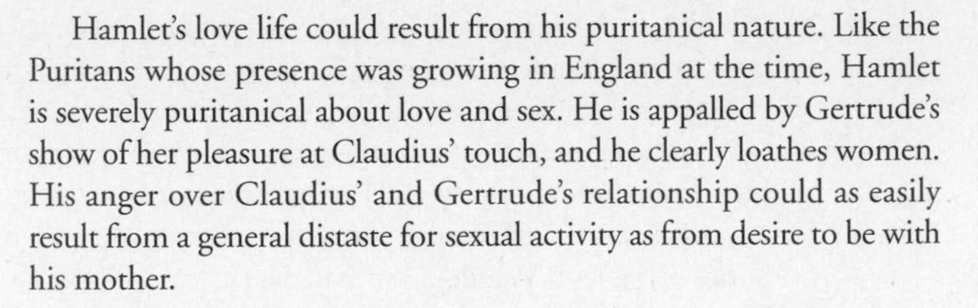

Hamlet's love life could result from his puritanical nature. Like the Puritans whose presence was growing in England at the time, Hamlet is severely puritanical about love and sex. He is appalled by Gertrude's show of her pleasure at Claudius' touch, and he clearly loathes women. His anger over Claudius' and Gertrude's relationship could as easily result from a general distaste for sexual activity as from desire to be with his mother.

Hamlet could be, at heart, a brutal misogynist, terrified of love because he is terrified of women. He verbally abuses Ophelia, using sexual innuendo and derision, and he encourages her to get to a nunnery. Another play on words, nunnery, in this instance, symbolizes both sexual abstinence and sexual perversity. In a cloister, Ophelia would take a vow of chastity, and in a brothel, she would serve as the basest sexual object.

Can concluding whether Hamlet is mad or merely pretending madness determine all the questions about Hamlet's nature? Could a madman manipulate his destiny as adeptly as Hamlet turns the tables on Rosencrantz and Guildenstern? Perhaps he is crazy like a fox . . . calculated and criminal. Or perhaps his own portrayal of madness—his "antic disposition"—that he dons like a mask or a costume actually drives him.

Could Hamlet's madness be his tragic flaw? Or is his flaw that he believes he is pretending to be mad? Are words his tragic flaw? Or could his tragic flaw be that he possesses the same hubris that kills all the great tragic heroes—that be believes he can decide who should live and who should die, who should be forgiven and who should be punished? Then, perhaps, is the Ghost a manifestation of his own conscience and not a real presence at all?

Which leads to the question students must ultimately consider: Is Hamlet a tragic hero at all? The Greek philosopher Aristotle defined the tragic hero with Oedipus as the archetype: a great man at the pinnacle of his power who, through a flaw in his own character, topples, taking everyone in his jurisdiction with him. Hamlet has no great power, though it is clear from Claudius' fears and from Claudius' assessment of Hamlet's popularity that he might have power were he to curry it among the people. His topple results as much from external factors as from his own flaws. Nevertheless, he certainly does take everyone with him when he falls.

Perhaps, like Arthur Miller, who redefined tragedy in an essay called "Tragedy and the Common Man," Shakespeare modified Aristotle's definition for his own age and created a tragic hero who can appeal to a larger, more enduring segment of the population. Hamlet fulfills the Aristotelian requirement that the tragic hero invoke in us a deep sense of pity and fear, that we learn from him how not to conduct our lives. Hamlet is our hero because he is, as we are, at once both confused and enticed by endless dilemmas that come from being, after all, merely human.

Claudius

Shakespeare's villains are complex. Unlike the earlier antiheroes of the revenge or morality plays that were popular in Elizabethan and Jacobean culture, Shakespearean criminals lack the simple clarity of absolute evil. Claudius is a perfect example of a quintessential Shakespearean antagonist.

Claudius is socially adept, and his charm is genuine. He can exhibit deep distress over his "dear brother's death" and admiration for his wife, "Th'imperial jointress to this warlike state." He knows the value of a great funeral, but quickly turns mourning into celebration and moves on "With mirth in funeral and with dirge in marriage" to whatever lies ahead. He is a decisive man, fair in his politics and commanding— if Gertrude's allegiance is any indication— in his bedroom.

The Queen has chosen to marry Claudius, and she defends him even to her son. In fact, she never opposes Claudius in anything. Were he dark and sinister in all things, she would fear and despise him; she follows him willingly even when he arranges to send her beloved son into the jaws of death. He must be sincere in his love for her. He explains his feelings for her at the end of Act IV, but he has proven these feelings consistently throughout the play

> The Queen his mother
> Lives almost by his looks, and for myself,
> My virtue or my plague, be it either which,
> She's so conjunctive to my life and soul
> That as the star moves not but in his sphere,
> I could not by her.

A character who loves is not merely a cold-blooded killer. Like Hamlet, his conflicting imperatives tear him apart.

Whereas he recognizes that his "offense is rank" and "smells to heaven," he also admits that he will not make amends with God because he refuses to give up what his crime has bought him. He is willing to take the consequences of his actions.

In some ways, Claudius exhibits more heroism than Hamlet. He manipulates fortune and takes what is not rightfully his, but remains unapologetic for his actions; he possesses enough strength to admit that he would do the same again. Hamlet, torn by conscience to smite the morally deficient Claudius, causes the death of six innocent people before he accomplishes his goal. By taking full responsibility for his actions, Claudius mitigates his evil nature.

The mark of a great Shakespearean antagonist is how completely he mirrors the protagonist. Claudius is no more Machiavellian than Hamlet; both ultimately believe that the end justifies the means, and both ultimately sacrifice humanity and humaneness in the acquisition of their goals.

What makes Claudius a villain is that he is wrong, and Hamlet is right. Claudius is a sneak who murdered and lied. Hamlet commits his murders in the open and suffers the pangs of his own conscience. Claudius subverts his conscience and refuses to ask for divine forgiveness. Hamlet seeks contrition and absolves himself of guilt before he dies; Claudius receives no absolution and seeks none. Hamlet will spend eternity in heaven; Claudius will burn in hell.

Gertrude

Gertrude is a shadowy character with little substance on which to hang a characterization. We can examine her through what others say about her more than through what she says.

That she is "th'imperial jointress" to the throne of Denmark indicates that she wields some power and suggests that Claudius' decision to marry her had political implications. Yet Hamlet indicts all women by calling her fickle—"frailty, thy name is woman." We see through Hamlet the picture of a woman who one day lived obediently and in the shadow of one king to whom she was devoted. The next day she allies herself in love and politics with the polar opposite of the man she formerly called husband.

The most haunting questions about Gertrude's character revolve around whether she knows that Claudius is a criminal. Is she merely a dependent woman who needs to live through her man? Is she a conniving temptress who used her power to conspire with Claudius to kill King Hamlet and usurp Prince Hamlet's ascendancy?

No textual references are conclusive. The Ghost of King Hamlet calls her his "most seeming virtuous queen." He entreats Hamlet to "Leave her to Heaven / And to those thorns that in her bosom lodge / To prick and sting her." These words could imply that she has reason to be guilty, that she is not blameless. Later, the Ghost implores Hamlet to comfort her. "But look, amazement on thy mother sits. / Oh step between her and her fighting soul." Again, he waxes protective of her but implies that she has some reason to be spiritually conflicted.

When Rosencrantz and Guildenstern arrive at Elsinore, she tells them that they have been sent for because of the way Hamlet "hath talked of you," and she promises them compensation fit for " a king's remembrance." She exhibits apparent sincerity in her concern for Hamlet, and yet, even after Hamlet has told her what he knows about Claudius, even after he has shared his fears of the trip to England, even after Hamlet has clearly proven that something is rotten in the state of Denmark, she never opposes Claudius to protect Hamlet. Unless, as some critics believe, she drinks the poisoned wine as an act of maternal protectiveness. Does she know the wine is poisoned? When "the Queen carouses to thy fortune, Hamlet" is she deliberately drinking to prevent Hamlet's death?

If Gertrude has overheard Claudius and Laertes plotting, she would know all. If she is in Claudius' confidence, she would be complicit with all his conspiracies. Though Claudius professes love and admiration for Gertrude, he never confides to anyone the extent of their relationship. Gertrude describes her love for Hamlet when she asks him not to return to Wittenberg. When she shares with Ophelia her hope that the young woman would have married her Hamlet, she divulges her wish for his happiness. However, she never declares any kind of emotion for Claudius, either positive or negative.

Ultimately, Gertrude's character remains malleable. In the hands of an astute actor and a clever director, she can come across as either Claudius' co-conspirator or Hamlet's defender. Either interpretation works, if built substantially.

Polonius

Casting Polonius in a demeaning light is a common danger. While he is a blowhard, and he does spout aphorisms that were, even in the 16th century, clichés, his clichés constitute sound advice and his observations prove themselves prophetic.

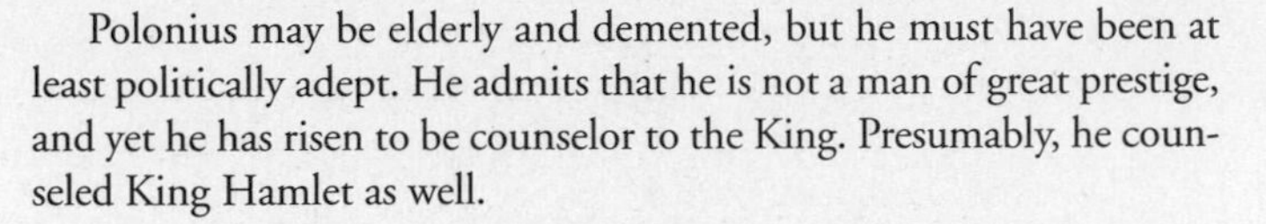

Polonius may be elderly and demented, but he must have been at least politically adept. He admits that he is not a man of great prestige, and yet he has risen to be counselor to the King. Presumably, he counseled King Hamlet as well.

An actor portraying Polonius should address the question of whether he is a devoted father or a ruthless politician. Does he sacrifice Ophelia to his ambitions and/or his fear of being discarded by the King? Does he send Reynaldo to spy on Laertes because he cares about his son, or is he worried about what Laertes' possible behavior might reflect back on his own character? Is he more concerned with his position in Denmark than with the welfare of his children? Is he then the victim of his own contrivances?

Ophelia

Ophelia is a difficult role to play because her character, like Gertrude's, is murky. Part of the difficulty is that Shakespeare wrote his female roles for men, and there were always limitations on them that restricted and defined the characterizations devised. In the case of an ingenue like Ophelia, a very young and lovely woman, Shakespeare would have been writing for a boy. The extent to which a boy could grasp subtle nuances might have prevented the playwright from fleshing out the character more fully.

We do know that Ophelia is torn between two contradictory poles. Her father and brother believe that Hamlet would use her, that he would take her virginity and throw it away because she could never be his wife. Her heart has convinced her that Hamlet loved her, though he swears he never did. To her father and brother, Ophelia is the eternal virgin, the vessel of morality whose purpose is to be a dutiful wife and steadfast mother. To Hamlet, she is a sexual object, a corrupt and deceitful lover. With no mother to guide her, she has no way of deciphering the contradictory expectations.

Just like Hamlet, the medieval precept that the father's word is unquestionable governs Ophelia. But her Renaissance sense of romantic love also rules her. How can she be obedient to her father and true to her love? When she lies to Hamlet and tells him that Polonius is home when he is concealed in the room eavesdropping, Ophelia proves she cannot live in both worlds. She has chosen one, and her choice seals her fate.

The dilemma also forces her into madness. She has no way to reconcile the contradictory selves her men demand that she be and still retain an equilibrium. In modern society, young women like Ophelia often become depressed or anorexic as a result of the conflicting demands; Ophelia's desperation literally drives her crazy, and she has no means with which to heal herself.

Laertes

Hamlet and Laertes presumably grew up together, fencing with one another and confiding in one another. Then Hamlet went away to Wittenberg and Laertes to Paris, parting the friendship. Still, Hamlet refers to Laertes as "a very noble youth."

Hamlet recognizes what Shakespeare has made abundantly clear throughout the play, that Laertes is Hamlet's foil. He mirrors Hamlet but behaves in the opposite manner. Where Hamlet is verbal, Laertes is physical; where Hamlet broods, Laertes blusters. Laertes' love for Ophelia and duty to Polonius drive him to passionate action, while Hamlet's love for Gertrude and duty to King Hamlet drive him to passionate inaction. In Laertes resides the picture of what Hamlet could be if the sound of his own words did not mesmerize him.

Horatio

Horatio epitomizes the faithful friend. He only questions Hamlet's judgment once, when Hamlet confides the fates of Rosencrantz and Guildenstern. Otherwise, Horatio supports every rash decision Hamlet makes.

Horatio is the man Hamlet wants to be. He is intelligent, but not driven by his intellectual creativity. Horatio seems to accept the world as it is handed to him where Hamlet is driven by his impulse question all apparent truths. (What T.S. Eliot calls "the energy to murder and create" in "The Love Song of J. Alfred Prufrock," a poem in which the the title character, paralyzed by words and feelings protests, "I am not Prince Hamlet. Nor was meant to be...") Marcellus and Bernardo Marcellus and Barnardo admire Horatio's intellect enough to want his opinion about the ghost, but no one accuses Horatio of talking or thinking too much. He can follow Hamlet's elaborate wordplays, but he is not inclined to engage in any. He knows enough to value what ignorance he has that can protect him from political ruin, but neither ambition nor deceit determines his loyalties.

Horatio loves Hamlet so much that he would rather impale himself on his own sword than live on after Hamlet's death. Hamlet passionately demonstrates his own deep love and admiration for Horatio in his request that Horatio tell Hamlet's story. Hamlet trusts his friend enough to leave him the task of finding the words that will divine the truth. For Hamlet, entrusting the task to Horatio declares his love better than expressing that love through any of Hamlet's poetry or philosophy. Action has at last spoken louder than words.

CRITICAL ESSAYS

On the pages that follow, the writer of this study guide provides critical scholarship on various aspects of Shakespeare's *Hamlet*. These interpretive essays are intended solely to enhance your understanding of the original literary work; they are supplemental materials and are not to replace your reading of *Hamlet*. When you're finished reading *Hamlet*, and prior to your reading this study guide's critical essays, consider making a bulleted list of what you think are the most important themes and symbols. Write a short paragraph under each bullet explaining why you think that theme or symbol is important; include at least one short quote from the original literary work that supports your contention. Then, test your list and reasons against those found in the following essays. Do you include themes and symbols that the study guide author doesn't? If so, this self test might indicate that you are well on your way to understanding original literary work. But if not, perhaps you will need to reread *Hamlet*.

Free Will and Fate in *Hamlet* and *Oedipus Rex*

The Classical tragedians appreciated the conflict between fate and free will. At the heart of every great tragedy lies the universal struggle between the human inclination to accept fate absolutely and the natural desire to control destiny. Both Sophocles and Shakespeare would agree that the forces of destiny and choice continually vie for control of human life. Yet, each of these great playwrights espouses a perspective on the struggle born of his specific time and culture. For the Greek Sophocles, fate far overpowers human will; the harder a man works to avoid his fate, the more surely he catapults forth into that very fate. Sophocles' characters ultimately surrender, after resistance, recognition, and reversal, to their destinies; Sophocles' plays warn against the pride that deceives us into believing we can alter fate through human intervention. For Shakespeare—a Christian—the choice between good and evil represents man's basic dilemma; for him, the human will is indomitable. Though fate may ultimately win, a man must fight to the death, if necessary, in order to remain the master of his own choices—choices that ultimately decide if and how his fate defeats him. The contrast between the two points of view is a note-worthy feature of any comparison between Sophocles' *Oedipus Rex* and Shakespeare's *Hamlet, Prince of Denmark.*

In his book *The Poetics,* Aristotle based the definition of tragedy on *Oedipus Rex,* making Sophocles' play the archetype of the genre. The notion that a hero must be a man of stature who is undone by some flaw in himself entirely governs Oedipus, the play's protagonist. While Oedipus only nominally controls his life, Hamlet's choices direct and ultimately destroy him. Oedipus, the prototypical Greek tragic hero, can see nothing until he blinds himself, thereby breaking free of the human compulsion to understand forces that one should simply obey. Introspection is only possible for Oedipus when his blindness forces him to stop examining the world around him. Sophocles' hero is stoic, strong, and stubborn; he seeks to bully fate and then gives in to self-destruction. Only then can he recognize his shortcomings and failures.

By contrast, Hamlet remains painfully aware of himself, his shortcomings, and his powerlessness to right what he perceives to be great wrongs. Poetic, thoughtful, and philosophical, he seeks to thwart his fate through intellectual maneuvering. Hamlet sees all too clearly the varying shades of gray that muddy his vision and blur his choices. He resembles the modern tragic hero—the common man tossed in a turbulent sea of social ills who loses his battle to correct them. He is bound inside himself, imprisoned by the words in his head that allow him no sleep, and no rest. " . . . There is nothing either good or bad but thinking makes it so," he says, surrendering to his obsessive thoughts. Hamlet is the quintessential Shakespearean hero, born of stature but not necessarily powerful, and undone by external forces as much as by internal ones. The struggle to live between opposing expectations and to assuage a throbbing conscience constitutes the battle Hamlet cannot win. No one force determines the outcome for Hamlet. God asks of him one thing, and man demands another.

Oedipus, however, remains at the singular mercy of the gods. Having learned from the oracle that he would kill his father and marry his mother, Oedipus has blundered into his own fate. Despite his best efforts to thwart the prophecy, dramatic irony prevails. Liberating Thebes from the tyranny of the Sphinx, Oedipus completes the first part of the dreaded prophecy. Flattered that the people choose him to be their king, Oedipus blindly accepts their offer of Jocasta's hand in marriage. Thus he completes the second phase of the prophecy by marrying his natural mother. Oedipus finalizes his destruction by attempting to escape it. By exerting his free will, he submits himself to the whim of destiny.

Oedipus eventually resigns himself to his failure by saying, "Oh God! It has come true. Light let this be the last time I see you." Having accepted his powerlessness, the only recourse left to him is to blind himself so that he may symbolically escape his failure. Unlike the Christian tragic hero, nothing motivates Oedipus to change the course of his life or make amends. He has disobeyed the gods by exhibiting too much pride, and he must now acquiesce to the will of the gods and accept his punishment. He travels to Colonnus and dies in exile, satisfied that he deserves such an end. In *Oedipus Rex,* man loses the battle for control of life and must surrender to the inescapable whims of fortune. The gods sit on Mount Olympus and manipulate humanity as though they were clay dolls to be moved about, discarded, and broken—like chess pieces. After Oedipus willingly acknowledges his insignificance, he attains the freedom to live beyond his pain and to die in peace.

For Hamlet, the consummate Christian tragic hero, fate exists, but human choices may cancel its power. Hamlet never stops choosing the paths he will take. Furthermore, his reluctance to succumb to his

fate stems as much from his religious morality as from his intellectual meandering. He is aware that his father's Ghost expects him to commit murder, that the Bible dictates that murder is wrong, even when executing an evil man, and that fate desires him to violate his God's Ten Commandments.

In *Hamlet,* King Hamlet's Ghost, who appears to Hamlet and directs him to punish Claudius, personifies fate. The Ghost reveals that Claudius, by killing his own brother, has committed a "murder most foul" and deserves to die. Hamlet can choose to obey his fate or ignore it and then face the consequences. Hamlet consistently avoids making this choice by refusing to act. However, his need for self-determination, driven by his psychological conflicts, finally forces him to take vengeance into his own hands. He finds that the forces of the primal world (which value "an eye for an eye") and the enlightened world (which legislate "Thou shalt not kill") equally compel him. The Ghost has ordered Hamlet to act against his conscience, and the diametrically opposed commands paralyze him.

In Oedipus, the king's corruption has bred an illness among his subjects. A plague has descended upon Thebes, and only Oedipus' punishment and removal will rectify the ills that are killing the people. Oedipus knows that he can right all only by excising the enemy of the gods from the body of the city-state. He is that enemy, having had the arrogance to assume that he could choose his own path.

On the other hand, a corrupt society that threatens to compromise his integrity confronts Hamlet. The King and his cohorts drink too much, and gamble too frequently. King Claudius casts on all of Denmark the reputation of an indolent wastrel. Hamlet knows that the duty to correct the depravity that holds his country captive falls to him, but he also knows that, in order to right this wrong, he must commit the worst of all crimes. He is torn between doing God's work and doing God's bidding, and the lines of distinction are not clearly recognizable. Were he able to simply reverse his will and submit to fate, he would find peace more swiftly; but constantly exercising his human will is Hamlet's cross to bear, and he only finds peace in death. Even making no choice exercises his free will, because inaction is as much a choice as action. Hamlet cannot ask God to absolve him of choice because the Christian God requires freely chosen submission. Where Oedipus must relinquish his will and allow the gods to manipulate him, Hamlet must exercise his will and follow as his God guides him.

Hamlet is an intellectual. He rationalizes his life and all its events and accepts nothing without careful analysis. The powers of Mount Olympus, however, entirely manipulate Oedipus. Hamlet can blame neither God nor fate. No unseen hand directs Hamlet's life and death; his own free will determines the results. As Oedipus exemplifies the Greeks' religious conviction that man is a pawn to the gods, Hamlet illustrates the Christians' fervent belief that man's mind is the master of self and chooses to follow God.

Neither Hamlet nor Oedipus has the last word in the argument between free will and fate. So long as humans have the power of thought, this concern will dominate literature. The preoccupation with the way in which the two vie for control of the human psyche promises to keep philosophy and art alive with myriad possibilities.

Ophelia's Dilemma

Although Gertrude says the branch broke and swept Ophelia down the river, the church denies her a full Christian burial on the grounds that she killed herself.

Prevailing wisdom is that one of two things is at work here: Either an inconsistency in Shakespeare's writing, which is not uncommon—his other works are fraught with them, though *Hamlet* far less than most. Or Shakespeare decided to up the ante on Hamlet's guilt. Gertrude could have not known the whole truth when she reported to Laertes and Claudius. She might have been trying to spare Laertes or to diffuse another tantrum on his part. The placement of the priest's admonition supports the suicide pretty solidly. So why did Ophelia do it?

Is Ophelia driven mad by her love for Hamlet, or is she the victim of a society that has created impossible expectations for its women? Had she the license to think for herself, Ophelia might have reasoned through her dilemma, but, caught as she is between her father's and brother's restrictive instructions and Hamlet's crushing demands, trapped as she is in a choice-less existence, Ophelia has no alternative but to throw herself into the river to drown.

From the start, Ophelia must define herself by male judgments that may be entirely miscalculated. Laertes warns her in her first scene onstage that Hamlet is merely trifling with her, that she is not of high enough station to warrant his true affection.

For Hamlet and the trifling of his favor
Hold it a fashion and a toy in blood,
A violet in the youth of primy nature,
Forward not permanent, sweet not lasting,
The perfume and suppliance of a minute,
No more.

Laertes goes on to tell Ophelia that while Hamlet might "love you now," he "is subject to his birth." Hamlet may not, "as unvalued persons do" choose his own mate. Hamlet is subject to the desires of his state, and he will necessarily break her heart. Should Ophelia relinquish her virginity to Hamlet, she would undoubtedly be shamed. A brother's expectation is that his sister is chaste, that she has no worth of her own except in her sex.

Polonius asks Ophelia what her relationship with Hamlet is, whether the young man has made advances to her. She answers that Hamlet has told her he loves her and that she believes him. Polonius calls her a "green girl," accusing her of being too naive to judge Hamlet's sincerity. Ophelia pleads with her father, "I do not know, my lord, what I should think." Her father instructs her not to think, to remain a virgin lest she shame her father.

Polonius has just told his son, "To thine own self be true." Yet he has negated any possibility that Ophelia might own her own self, that she might have a will apart from her men. The father offers no such choice to his daughter.

Women of Ophelia's time were trained to be chattel to their men. They were taught needlecraft, righteousness of character, servitude. But they were not encouraged to write or read or reason. The assumption that both Laertes and Polonius make is that Ophelia is a virgin, that she is theirs to sell to a husband for the bride wealth she can garner.

Hamlet, on the other hand, accuses her of faithlessness, of whoring. He tells her to get her to a nunnery, a statement that implies that she is no better than a whore. When he meets her in the corridor and asks her where her father is, he knows she cannot answer. He knows Old Polonius is standing nearby, but she cannot reveal his whereabouts. Ophelia answers feebly, "At home, my lord," and her answer throws Hamlet into a frenzy because she has answered dishonestly. He has set her up. She has no other choice but to say that her father is at home; she is forced to lie and thereby to incur Hamlet's disapproval.

In her essay "The Warrant of Womanhood, Shakespeare and Feminist Criticism," Ann Thompson points out that male characters in Shakespeare have a limited perception of the female characters. Shakespeare, says Thompson, is sympathetic to women in this area; the playwright goes so far as to let his audience know that he intended for the male character to misunderstand the female, that the male character is often dead wrong about the female. The men completely misread their women, and the consequences are often tragic.

Such is Ophelia's case. Her men are wrong about her. They make assumptions and then they make demands based on those assumptions, but there is no way Ophelia can meet the demands because the underlying assumptions are flawed.

While she lives in the same patriarchal society that demands that she subjugate herself to her father and her brother until she is married, Ophelia has fallen in love with Prince Hamlet. There is strong evidence that she has even had sexual relations with him. Restricted by the dominating societal mores, Ophelia has engaged in a willful act that would ruin her family should it come to light. When her father dies at the hand of her lover, Ophelia is left guilty and alone.

Ophelia's mother is dead and, unlike so many Shakespearean heroines, Ophelia has no female alliances that might save her from the blindness of her male wardens. She is not clever enough to rationalize her behavior or to teach her men the lesson they would be forced to learn were they in a comedy. Her life is worthless because she has violated her code of ethics. She must die.

Men dominate Ophelia's world. But they are men who want too much and who represent too many contradictions. She cannot comply with their wills, and she cannot assert her own. She cannot live because her Selfhood does not exist.

CliffsNotes Review

Use this CliffsNotes Review to test your understanding of the original text, and reinforce what you've learned in this book. After you work through the review and essay questions, identify the quote section, and the fun and useful practice projects, you're well on your way to understanding a comprehensive and meaningful interpretation of Shakespeare's *Hamlet.*

Q&A

1. What is Hamlet's relationship with Ophelia at the play's beginning?

a. They are schoolmates.

b. They are cousins.

c. They are in love.

d. They have not met.

2. What is Hamlet trying to decide in his "To be" soliloquy?

a. If the ghost of his father is real

b. If his life is worth living

c. If he should murder Claudius in order to become king

d. If he should confront Gertrude about her rash remarriage

3. What is the main plot function that the players serve?

a. They help Hamlet determine if his father's ghost is telling the truth.

b. They distract Hamlet from his grief, which gives Claudius enough time to arrange for Hamlet's murder.

c. They instruct Gertrude regarding the true nature of her former husband's death.

d. They distract the court while Fortinbras's troops surround Elsinore.

4. Why does the apparition appear in Gertrude's chamber?

a. To prove to Gertrude that Hamlet is not mad.

b. To warn Gertrude that Claudius is a murderer.

c. To show Gertrude that she is forgiven for remarrying so quickly.

d. To protect Gertrude from Hamlet's excessive anger.

5. Who survives at the end of the play?

a. Ophelia

b. Gertrude

c. Rosencrantz and Guildenstern

d. Horatio

Answers (1) c. (2) b. (3) a. (4) d. (5) d.

Identify the Quote: Find Each Quote in *Hamlet*

1. Good-night, sweet prince,
And flights of angels sing thee to thy rest!

2. Madness in great ones must not unwatch'd go.

3. The lady doth protest too much methinks.

4. Neither a borrower, nor a lender be;
For loan oft loses both itself and friend,
And borrowing dulls the edge of husbandry.

5. Something is rotten in the state of Denmark.

Answers (1) The speaker is Horatio in Act V, Scene 2. The statement is directed at Hamlet's corpse. (2) The speaker is Claudius in Act III, Scene 1, addressing Polonius. (3) The speaker is Gertrude in Act III, Scene 2. Gertrude says this line to Hamlet during *The Mousetrap* in response to Hamlet's question, "Madam, how like you this play?" (4) The speaker is Polonius in Act I, Scene 3. Polonius is giving Laertes departing advice on how to live and how to act. (5) The speaker is Marcellus in Act I, Scene 4. The listener is Horatio. Marcellus, Horatio, and Hamlet have just seen the ghost. The appearance of ghosts or other supernatural phenomena were believed to be an indication of impending doom for the whole country.

Essay Questions

1. What kind of a King is Claudius? What evidence shows the kind of monarch he is and the kind of man he is? Is this his appearance, or is it his true character?

2. What is Hamlet's conflict over the Ghost's existence? Why does he continue to doubt the "honesty" of the Ghost even after Claudius confesses his guilt?

3. Name the various foils Shakespeare has created for Hamlet. Why is each important to the play?

4. Explain the function of the Gravediggers at the beginning of Act V.

5. Find examples of Hamlet's voices as he speaks as ________________

   The avenger

   The philosopher, unemotional reasoner

   The actor, self-critical and self-directed

   The ironic observer

   The disgusted observer, bemoaning the hopelessness of the human condition

   The indecisive man desperate to be decisive

6. Look through the text and find five questions that drive the theme, characters, or plot of the play. Explain why the questions are important and why Shakespeare poses them as questions and not as answers.

7. Explain the effect Hamlet's ideas of sin and salvation have on the development of his character and the movement of the plot.

8. Identify the three revenge plots in Hamlet, and explain why each is important to the development of the play.

Practice Projects

1. Stage the final scene in Hamlet, paying special attention to how you place the bodies of the falling dead on the stage. Why would you choose to place them thus?

2. Conduct a mock jury trial to prove whether Hamlet is or is not mad.

3. Conduct a mock jury trial to prove that Gertrude is an accomplice in the death of King Hamlet.

4. Watch the film *Rosencrantz and Guildenstern are Dead.* What does the film tell you about these two men? After seeing them from this new perspective, what do you think of them? Has your opinion of them changed? How does playwright Tom Stoppard's interpretation compare to Shakespeare's portrayal of them?

CliffsNotes Resource Center

The learning doesn't need to stop here. CliffsNotes Resource Center shows you the best of the best—links to the best information in print and online about the author and/or related works. And don't think that this is all we've prepared for you; we've put all kinds of pertinent information at `www.cliffsnotes.com`. Look for all the terrific resources at your favorite bookstore or local library and on the Internet. When you're online, make your first stop `www.cliffsnotes.com` where you'll find more incredibly useful information about Shakespeare's *Hamlet.*

Books and Articles

This CliffsNotes book, published by Wiley Publishing, Inc., provides a meaningful interpretation of Shakespeare's *Hamlet.* If you are looking for information about the author and/or related works, check out these other publications:

Andrews, Richard and Rex Gibson, editors. *Cambridge School Shakespeare.* Cambridge University Press, Cambridge, England, 1985. A lively interpretive mix of production, perspective, and academic investigation.

Bevington, David, Editor. *Twentieth Century Interpretations of Hamlet.* Prentice Hall Spectrum Books, 1968. A collection of essays exploring the various aspects of *Hamlet* from character to syntax.

Doyle, John and Ray Lischner. *Shakespeare For Dummies.* Foster City IDG Books Worldwide, Inc., 1999. This guide to Shakespeare's plays and poetry provides summaries and scorecards for keeping track of who's who in a given play, as well as painless introductions to language, imagery, and other often intimidating subjects.

Halliday, F.E. *A Shakespeare Companion.* Penguin Press, 1952. A comprehensive dictionary of Shakespeare's life and works.

Holderness, Graham, editor. *The Shakespeare Myth.* St. Martin's Press, New York, 1988. Postmodern revisionist view of the cultural politics of studying the work of William Shakespeare.

Levi, Peter. *The Life and Times of William Shakespeare.* Easy to read and full of interesting sociological commentary on the time period, this is as accurate a depiction of Shakespeare's life as one can expect.

Prosser, Eleanor. *Hamlet and Revenge.* Stanford University Press, 1968. Argues that Hamlet is a good Christian led astray by a jealous ghost.

It's easy to find books published by Wiley Publishing, Inc. You'll find them in your favorite bookstores (on the Internet and at a store near you). We also have three Web sites that you can use to read about all the books we publish

- `www.cliffsnotes.com`
- `www.dummies.com`
- `www.wiley.com`

Internet

Check out these Web resources for more information about William Shakespeare, *Hamlet,* and Shakespeare's other works

The Hamlet home page. `www.hamlet.edmonton.ab.ca` –This web site will guide users to links to many other interesting and helpful *Hamlet* Web pages.

The Hamlet Navigator. `www.clicknotes.comhamnavl/Hhome.html`—This colorful and informative site provides summaries of the plays's acts and scenes, gives notes on the characters, and explains themes and language. Includes a word search program.

Falcon Education Link Home Page and Shakespeare Resource. `www.falconedlink.com/~falcon`—This fun and accessible resource provides thorough explanations and descriptions.

Hamlet Notes. `www.glen-net.ca/english/hamlet.html`—This link can connect you to several other *Hamlet* sites, including discussions titled "Hamlet's Character," "Hamlet Discussion," "Hamlet's Flaw and the Question of Delay," and "Hamlet's Delay." The link called "To be or not to be" provides an excellent analysis of Hamlet's most famous soliloquy, and it includes questions for further study.

A Short Course on Shakespeare's Hamlet. `http//server1/hypermart.net/hamlet`—This site provides a complete overview of the play, its characters, themes, and language, along with wonderful pictures. Click on the "Course" link to access an online edition of *Hamlet* with more explanatory notes, questions and answers, and other useful study guides.

Shakespeare Illustrated. `www.cc.emory.edu/ENGLISH`—This site provides high quality reproductions of paintings from nineteenth-century Shakepearean productions. The plays are listed alphabetically, so users can click on the play they are interested in and get pictures with detailed discussion and analysis.

Surfing with the Bard. `www.ulen.som/Shakespeare`—Described as "Your Shakespeare classroom on the Internet," this site provides the user with links to terrific *Hamlet* sites. Besides that, there are seven different "Zones," each one carefully designed to make sure that you get the most out of all of Shakespeare's plays.

Hamlet. `www.pathguy.com/hamlet`—Designed by a pathologist with a passion for *Hamlet,* this colorful, informative, and always up-to-date site contains illustrations and explanations that bring *Hamlet* to life and explain the play in modern, conversational language. The section called "Background" provides interesting insights into character and motivation.

Films

Hamlet. Directed by and starring Kenneth Branagh. Castle Rock Entertainment, 1996. Kenneth Branagh made the courageous decision not to shorten the Second Quarto / Folio text from which this film is adapted. He also decided not to modernize the language. An excellent and complete film version that is faithful to the Second Quarto text.

Hamlet. Directed by and starring Laurence Olivier. Denham Studios, 1948. This stark, abstract, deeply psychological black-and white film earned four Academy Awards. Somewhat dated, but still very good.

Hamlet. Directed by Tony Richardson. Woodfall, 1969. The first film version to use elements of the First Quarto in the script, this film is an adaptation of a London theatrical production. Uniquely entertaining.

Hamlet. Directed by Franco Zeffirelli, starring Mel Gibson. Warner Bros., 1990. Zefferelli's realistic Elsinore and Danish coast lend this film a gutsy realism while capturing the essence of *Hamlet.* Passionate and easy to understand, the action never slows in this sumptuous film.

Rosencrantz and Guildenstern Are Dead. Directed by Tom Stoppard. Buena Vista, 1990. This movie, based on the play of the same name, is written from the perspective of Hamlet's two quirky, comical school chums. Their story weaves in and out of Shakespeare's play.

However, Stoppard chooses to make the men and their dilemma a comedy rather than a tragedy. Highly entertaining.

Send Us Your Favorite Tips

In your quest for knowledge, have you ever experienced that sublime moment when you figure out a trick that saves time or trouble? If you've discovered a useful tip that helped you understand Shakespeare's *Hamlet* more effectively and you'd like to share it, the CliffsNotes staff would love to hear from you. Go to our Web site at `www.cliffsnotes.com` and click the Talk to Us button. If we select your tip, we may publish it as part of CliffsNotes Daily, our exciting, free e-mail newsletter. To find out more or to subscribe to the newsletter, go to `www.cliffsnotes.com` on the Web.

Index

G

H

I

J

K

L

M

N

O

P

Q

R

S

T

U

V

W

Y

NOTES

NOTES

NOTES

NOTES

NOTES